MW00454121

The Imprinted Survivor

Susan Steen Ciolek

Susan Steen Ciolek
"Help spread the Word"

Copyright © 2012 Susan Ciolek

First edition. All rights reserved. No part of this book may be reproduced in any form, except for the inclusion of brief quotations in a review, without permission in writing from the author or publisher.

Chapter opening font: Celtasmigoria

To order additional copies, please contact:
susansteenciolek@ymail.com

Special thanks to the Congregation of the Marians of the Immaculate Conception for permission to reprint photos on p. 32 and 33 and quotations of St. Faustina.

DIARY, Saint Maria Faustina Kowalska: Divine Mercy in My Soul © 1987 Congregation of the Marians of the Immaculate Conception, Stockbridge, MA 01263. All Rights Reserved. Reprinted with permission.

Manufactured in the United States of America

"Man can live about forty days without food,
about three days without water,
about eight minutes without air,
but only one second without hope."

—Unknown

For my children: Sarah, Abagael, and Frances,
whose patience, along with their father's,
I happily dedicate this book to.

Contents

Preface

The ability to survive doesn't always follow statistics. It can be one of those unexplainable possibilities that God has graced us with called miracles. All things may become real with God's will and our ability to recognize that which we have been blessed. This reality is not always possible if you do not use what you have been given to its fullest. Feel blessed in your experiences. Take from them what you can use to forge forward and give back of yourself.

This book is a combination memoir of my experiences in life and its battles with cancer, my father's memories during WWII, and my ancestral lineage. It holds within its creative narration stories as told by my grandmother of her time as a household servant for Princess Beatrice, the youngest child of Queen Victoria. Memory should be, but is not always, reliable; for this reason, please be assured that every effort was made to research and when possible provide documentation. These stories have their basis in oral tradition or historical fact, but can at times have a creative element when viewed through the eyes and ears of my grandparents, parents, and myself. They have been passed down in some cases over a period of 100-plus years.

1

I Should Have Died but I Survived

fter waging three battles with cancer over a five-year period and beating all the odds, I came to realize that there had to be something unique in my journey that I must seek out and share. This path uncovered an imprint or a personal road map, a map that many may relate to and gain insight from.

I learned that our personality transmits a pattern of energy that is uniquely our own. We are born with a distinct biological genetic coding. This pattern or code is imprinted in our brain and determines how our brain develops. These inherent personality and behavioral traits remain with us throughout our life and influence how we act and think.

Our imprint influences who we become while controlling and motivating our lives. Writing this book has allowed me to fulfill an inner desire to seek out my own personal imprint while I search for my unique connection to this huge sea of souls we call humanity. I wish to convey to you the part we all play in the bigger picture. Using my flair for story telling—or as my family would say, "my gift of gab"—I hope to lead you on an adventure through time by recounting my lineage in a series of events based on stories as they were told or researched. My intention is not to exclude or devalue ancestors who left their imprint upon my mind and soul without my knowledge. Nor is it to share facts altered through time and tale. It is my hope that the reader will gain an insight into what has transpired in my life, my thoughts, and my actions as I faced the physical and emotional turmoil of a critical illness, an illness that should have ended my life thirteen years ago.

I do not hold a degree in psychology. My knowledge is based on research, soul searching, and life's lessons as I battled against cancer and won. I will relate the havoc the disease created in my inner self. This battle changed the way I viewed life and prompted me to answer the question I have been asked over and over, "How did you have the strength to keep fighting?" All around me, doctors were inquiring about my gene pool, looking for a genetic flaw linking me to the big "C" and finding none. However, I discovered another answer within myself. This answer led me to believe my inherent genetic trait wasn't a physical flaw, but a behavioral or personality trait that allowed me to find an inner strength to not "give up" or "give in," whichever you prefer. It led me to overcome what seemed to be a hopeless situation, especially if I had surrendered to statistics.

I remember one seasonably warm autumn day spent behind the glass, brick, and mortar walls of the Mayo

Clinic. One of our country's top oncologists asked me if I understood how unbelievably lucky I was to have survived. I already knew at that point it wasn't luck at all, but strength and faith. Be it inherited or learned, it worked. I once read somewhere that luck is where faith in God meets inner strength. I hope you will gain an inner confidence and knowledge in yourself after sharing in my search with me.

Through hours of research, this book evolved and came to include findings dealing with the word 'imprint' as the basis or root of which we are formed from generations past. Developed through many and varied experiences, our imprint is formed. About midway through *The Imprinted Survivor,* I discovered the term "epigenetic marks." These marks are the imprints left on our genetic material due to environmental and psychological conditions. These genetic imprints may pass new traits through the genes but may not alter the genetic code. This evolving imprint is then passed down through the lineage of generations. This connection has been also supported by self-help specialists and psychologists, and is now linked to medical science.

During my journey, as I waged a war for survival, I always believed that my inner voice was so important to listen to and heed. You know yourself better than anyone. Once you realize that your experiences connect with your individual imprint, you can face any battle as a proud warrior.

This book is my gift to you and anyone who is battling life's struggles. Writing it allowed me to pursue a new mode of creative expression. In my past thirty-odd years as an artist, I had limited my inner self or imprint to the use of canvas to express myself, paint and brush to convey my emotional and physical experiences, producing in my paintings a representation of my personal life. Now using my laptop and words I hope to reach many more survivors and caregivers. If you are currently struggling, do not say, "But I cannot call myself a survivor yet, for I am still battling the challenge," be it inner conflict or physical illness. You are a survivor because you are here today to read my words; and we all are still battling struggles in life each and every day. As long as our hearts are beating we are survivors in this lifetime. Our endurance and survival adds value to our imprint for generations to come.

Thoughts that try to fully embrace facing death, whether they concern yourself or another human being, affect us by creating meaning in our present life and the ties that bind us to the past. After my mother's death, I searched back into my roots for my personal connection. I found reality in my lineage to which I could link an imprint to the personality traits one finds in a survivor.

2

The Journey Begins

February 2010

I knelt at the foot of the bed in our master bedroom in front of an ornate wooden chest, pondering the Pandora's box I was about to open. Painted with an intricate floral design, the chest is straight out of the early 1900s. I removed the pile of a dozen or so magazines and books that had accumulated on top, some half read with corners dog-eared. Then, folding the old pair of jeans and sweatshirt I had hurriedly wiggled into the night the call came from Constable House, I remembered that moment eight days before at two o'clock in morning, when the phone startled me from a sound sleep.

Carefully, I lifted the lid, gazing inside; I remembered the chest was lined in cedar as the scent rose to my nostrils. This chest belonged to my Aunt Amy, who had raised my mother; it was an inherited heirloom that was passed down to me many years before. Called a hope chest, it was used to store a young woman's treasured items until her wedding day. My chest now held baby pictures, christening outfits, school report cards, one neatly folded American flag that covered my father's casket, a bound maternal Manning Family Tree, a Bible, an old photo album, and a very large manila envelope covered with Dad's writing.

Sue,

Important Family Papers
Steen and Gaffney lineage—put in safe place.

Love, Dad

A week before, on February first, Mom passed away at age ninety-two. She lived a long, full life. As her only child, I sat alone with no brothers or sisters to share in this parental grief. Searching through the treasures stored in my chest, I thumbed through my father's papers and turned the pages of the Manning Family Tree, realizing for the first time in my life that any questions I might have wanted to ask my parents about their lives and those of my grandparents may be lost in time forever.

It was one of those bone-chilling winter days with a steel gray sky blanketing our small Midwestern town. A few snowflakes gently floated in the air, catching on the summer's late-blooming cone flowers and mums I had neglectfully not cut back with the arrival of an early snow. The dead blooms now added their own texture to an otherwise dull winter landscape in my garden. Wrapping my favorite afghan around my shoulders, the one that had kept me company during my battles with the big "C," I headed for the cozy chair by the fire with my family tree, Bible, and Dad's envelope. The house had a lonely silence about it, one that left me in a melancholy state as the kids were away at school and Joe was in Cleveland on business. Our family dog Philomena, a furry mixed breed, was curled up on her pillow by the hearth, letting the warmth of the fire soothe her arthritic back haunches. She gave me a forlorn look that said, "I need some attention." In all the activity throughout the past week with funeral arrangements, she had been the ever-faithful neglected family member. Scooping her up onto my lap, I nestled into my chair to study the treasures the old chest had stored over the past thirty-some years.

I would spend the next two days calling cousins and one very dear aunt in her nineties to whom I always linked my artistic ability. I sought to find answers to all sorts of questions and stories I had been told in my younger years when I spent endless evenings on Aunt Amy's back porch in Pennsylvania. There I listened to my aunt and uncle tell stories about Drury's Run and the coalmines. Now clouded in memories, I hoped these newly exhumed artifacts might shed some light on my family's history. Between its pages, the Bible contained cards and notes from well-wishers during my first battle with cancer. Within the yellowed pages of the Manning Family Tree were names, dates, and stories dating back to 1634 when the family settled in New Throne, now Cambridge, after traveling from England. Dad's envelope held pictures and letters from my father's sister, Mollie, sent to him with scribbled notes of family history. Some letters even sported the royal crests of Kensington Palace and Clarence House, signed by Minnie Cochrane, Princess Beatrice's Lady-in-Waiting. These items spoke of times long gone in the early nineteenth century, when my grandmother had spent her days and nights on the Isle of Wight and in London, England serving the royal family and the throne. Filled with information, the letters led me to crusty history books covered in dust and yearning to be read from the shelves behind ivy-covered walls of university libraries. Stories filled the crispy, aged pages, telling of royalty trying to live lives far from the common man's view, yet suffering from the same ills that their subjects dealt with. They told of the same love, hate, sadness, diseases, joys, and envy that life dishes out to each of us.

My mother's death brought to the surface emotions I had held bottled up in my soul as I faced the end of the life that brought me into this world. Like an aged bottle of wine, the previous years fermented events of my battles to survive cancer within my memory. My experiences had formed a full-bodied flavor for life that I am now ready to pour out and share. I have finally chosen to drink from the glass of life steeped with emotion of my past experiences and those of my ancestors, as their blood flows deep red in hue through my veins, much like an aged merlot.

Stripping away the layers, cells, and genes to uncover elements lurking just below the surface, I craved the search with the zest of the past warrior. I recalled the fight with the deadly disease inside my body that had sought to take over my life. Fear nagged in the pit of my stomach, yet the curiosity burned holes in my will to keep the past in the past. Part of me was scared of what might linger in my family history. Would I uncover some long-held family secret that had been buried for years? Or would I find the answer to my survival?

I hope you will join me as I seek to share this journey through the struggles I endured to survive cancer and the lives my ancestors led to grace me with the existence I have been given. For if it were not for each of our ancestors' survival, you and I would not have been born. To this day, I still struggle and continue to go in for checkups, and have now recently learned that I am facing a new battle with meningioma brain tumors. This threat to my physical and mental state has spurred my need to put pen to paper for fear of complications from my current diagnosis. As the reader you will share in my experiences of battling a series of primary cancers as a young mother of three, then struggling through middle age as a woman of the sandwich generation caring for elderly parents, and finally facing over-the-hill with brain tumors and memory issues as my teenagers expound, "I told you Mom—don't you remember?" and I truthfully don't.

The unspoken fear that the cancer will return always persists; I am well aware that the treatment that may have saved my life was also carcinogenic. This shadow follows me wherever I go. Like an addict's battle with drugs or alcohol, it is always present. Rewarding myself a badge of courage after each healthy checkup reminds me of where I had been many years ago and how hard I have fought to be where I am today. These ongoing tests and follow-up appointments are still the hardest part of my present journey in remission and will be for the remainder of my life, but how wonderful it is that I have a life to live.

Realizing a need to pull myself out of the emotions buried in the depths of my soul, I became consumed in my writing. The process allowed me to face feelings I had been unwilling to deal with until this point. Through this creative expression, I was able to begin to heal and achieve some peace. Armed with my father's envelope, the Manning Family Tree, pictures, and letters of correspondence between himself and his sister, I started my journey by taking full advantage of the Internet. This endeavor proved challenging for someone of my generation. I had grown up reaching for the dictionary or encyclopedia, without the availability of spell check and Google. After the patience of some very dear friends, Marybeth and Mark, I only stumbled over two or three viruses in my research and took a flying leap into the purchase of a mini notebook. This new smaller version of my old laptop proved easier to transport to my favorite local coffee shop's corner table. There I hooked myself to a programmed Ipod my daughter Frannie had loaded with George Winston and classic Irish melodies, and proceeded to pound out these pages. Sporting my new mini and Ipod, I felt as if I had plugged into the new generation at a hip 50+.

The next step proved to be even more intriguing as I researched some information that could only be gathered at local and state college libraries, and the Memorial Continental Hall that housed my aunt's Daughters of the American Revolution papers. I also talked to one genealogist from Washington D.C., and a very helpful historian named Anne who encouraged me to e-mail a librarian in London, England, who is responsible for the archived letters of the royal family.

Being a person that is easily driven by a justifiable mission, I didn't ask myself why I was stricken with cancer, but why I survived. This grew to be the basis of a story I was destined to tell, not only to the readers of this book, but also myself from a different point of view. Losing a number of close friends and relatives to cancer within the past thirteen years of my life, I found myself surviving again and again. The piss and vinegar my mother was full of in her old age has obviously passed on to me and I wasn't giving up on finding the answer to my question of survival.

All the genetic findings of countless doctors could not prove any physical connection between my DNA and cancer. Although my ancestry provided no clues about why I became sick, would it offer evidence to how I survived? Could it be that an imprint in my personality traits, which many psychologists suggest can be passed through one's heredity or Selective Adaptation[1], helped me to survive? Had my mother and father and their faith given me the wonderful gift of strength to persevere? I will let you be the judge.

The remainder of this book will also reveal two vastly different worlds: the wealthy, influential family of my

[1] An evolutionary capability whereby one becomes better suited; also known as Darwinian fitness.

mother and the childhood my father faced as an immigrant. These two starkly contrasting family structures offer a glimpse into the past and the lives of people trying to deal with their own struggles and joys.

One family was forced to leave its homeland in the United Kingdom to immigrate to America while another family can trace its roots as far back as 1634, some 300-plus years earlier, when they settled in Cambridge, Massachusetts. Both families find themselves eventually intertwining in a small coal-mining town in the Allegheny Mountains of Pennsylvania. They use their own survival traits to deal with their experiences and personal battles in life.

Join me now as I travel back in time to search for an answer to my survival and possible link to my ancestral lineage and faith. I will begin this time warp I am about to undertake by asking the question, "Are survival traits learned or inherited?" Studies have shown that twins separated at birth can possess similar personality traits, thus supporting a theory of inherited traits. This observation has surfaced in my research for an inner ability, or imprint, to survive. Delving into my lineage of ancestors and their ability to form a strong conviction to persevere against adversity, while cultivating traits that I am graced with in my present life, I forge forward. I do not claim to be immune from self-pity as my life and faith has been challenged numerous times. Such was the case as I shared many beautiful moments with close friends and family as they passed from this earthy existence. I invite you now to enter my battles and the struggles of my family and friends.

3

The Diagnostic Trip

April 1, 1998

he year was 1998, Good Friday, and I was about to depart on a journey that would forever change my life, for nothing in nature ever stays the same. My family of three little girls and husband Joe were just settling into the new home we had built in a quaint, rural, Midwestern town complete with the picket fence and rose garden. Looking forward to the holiday weekend, I was making a quick stop to pick up some last-minute supplies for the girls' Easter Baskets and get to my three o'clock doctor's appointment. After countless appointments with a doctor who will remain nameless and x-rays at an equally nameless hospital, I ventured to a new physician with the hope of finding the source of my nagging cough and inability to effectively fight every cold or flu that came my way. Since I was mother to a seven, five, and two-year-old, it seemed I was always sick. During the appointment and subsequent x-ray, the physician discovered a possibly life-threatening illness growing inside of me. A small white dot about the size of a pea had appeared in the x-ray of my left lung, which raised the possibility of a cancerous lesion. For the next two months, each morning brought with it a sick feeling to my stomach as I lived in the impending reality of an illness that was unchanging throughout months of diagnostic tests. It was a place I found myself as the dawn broke each morning and the alarm clock sounded the familiar call to pack lunches, make breakfast, and get my two oldest daughters ready for school. I would roll out of bed, aware of the motherly duties my family relied upon that gave my life meaning as well. The familiar routine provided a place for my mind to retreat to as I tried to avoid what my future might have in store around the next bend on this road to a diagnosis.

Critical illness gives life a visible threshold from where it may end. At that location you are faced with finding a value to place on it. Are you happy? Or is there room for improvement in what your future may hold? As many of us find, there is. The reality of the future may be short or long, but there are no guarantees as there were none in the past. Yet, we do not usually ponder the loss of a future until some undeniable situation evolves. From this vantage point, fear can take over. The only certainty you have to confront is that inevitable reality and you need to fight like hell. Otherwise, the devil may claim your spirit, and you put your tail between your legs running in the opposite direction, or you cower helplessly.

Often, the not knowing is worse than the knowledge of illness, as most cancer victims admit. My physician ordered the customary CT to look for any form of calcification in the visible lesion positioned in my upper lobe of my left lung. A calcification might indicate the body's prior ability to seal off an earlier infection rather than the presence of a cancer. It was at this point I requested my own copy of the CT report as my impatience took over. For me this seemed to be a faster way to find out what was inside of my body, as waiting for the next step in this diagnostic chain to be scheduled was taking its toll on me. This was probably not the smartest idea. Driving home from the doctor's office on that April afternoon, when normally I would be out in the garden working on my annual spring clean, the word 'carcinoma,' printed on the CT report

Critical illness gives life a visible threshold from where it may end.

next to me on the passenger's seat, was branded into my brain as a cowhand brands a steer. I entered the empty house; my two older daughters were still at school and my youngest, one month away from turning three, was up the street at our neighbor's house, a very kind nurse who volunteered to watch Frannie during my errands that day. In the silence of the house my world came crashing down. I witnessed it before my eyes as if looking through a crystal ball—a future that might not exist at age forty-three.

I thought of my maternal grandmother, who had died at forty, leaving seven children motherless. Was history repeating itself? If it was, I became more driven from that moment on to prove it wrong. I also remembered the stories of strength and determination my paternal grandmother held while escaping the poverty of life as an Irish peasant and the air raids she faced during World War I in London alone with an infant and a toddler. The inner voice that whispered inside me would not accept these circumstances. I ventured up the street to retrieve Frannie. When Beth answered the door, she could read my expression and handled it as any professional nurse would. Supportive, but unable to answer all the questions that came spewing from my lips, I could see in her eyes the hurt from the medical knowledge she possessed. I then realized that what had only been bouncing around in my head was real and not a dream I could banish upon awakening.

At this point, my questions had to wait until I could talk to a specialist and create a battle plan to prepare for what seemed hopeless in the irrational state that came over me. I phoned my doctor's office requesting a return call. Luckily it came within the hour, along with a plan for an exploratory procedure he was in the process of scheduling.

Throughout critical illness you learn to deal with all sorts of medical professionals, some who may know their skill, but not the needs of human beings. When it comes to cancer, a heartfelt connection with your doctor is crucial to achieve a healthy relationship with a positive outcome. I will never forget one doctor who performed a procedure on me when the CT could not give a definitive result other than the possibility of a carcinoma. We met in the operating room after my kind and understanding family doctor went the extra mile to get this procedure scheduled quickly through his connections at the hospital. This exploratory procedure involved a tube being inserted down my nose to try and retrieve a biopsy from my lung. As I lay on the operating table prepped and drugged for the procedure, this doctor entered the room and I could sense the demeanor of the nurses and techs change in his presence. Approaching where I lay under numerous spotlights, he opened his mouth and out came an arrogant statement, which had no regard for my fears facing the possibility of the "Big C," let alone this procedure. He expounded, "I don't know who you know, but I never meet my patients in the operating room. They wait to get an appointment at my private office before surgery." There came the hint in the word 'private.' OK, Sir, I now understand your office appointments come with $$$. It didn't matter to him that I would have been kept in limbo another month trying to make an appointment, not to mention priceless days waiting for treatment that might save my life, but my family doctor did. "Thank you, Doc!"

While waiting for a diagnosis, my need to be around people became apparent. Being alone only let my mind drift to a place I did not want to go. Human beings were my primary distraction. The next came in the form of prayer and lastly, my love of gardening. At this point in my life, I was not as strong in my faith as I should have been. Like many Christians, I found prayer when I needed it. In this I must admit I was weak. Turning to prayer as I gardened transformed my yard into what I liked to call my Rosary Garden. Working in the soil, I prayed and experienced an offering in my efforts to achieve a fruitful and pleasing garden both aesthetically and within my soul.

At the beginning of this first cancer, my relationships soon became strained as I waited for test results. The cancer was not yet confirmed. I had trouble eating and sleeping and could not even make any plans other than doctor and test appointments. The children felt the stress; Joe and I, with no relatives living nearby, sought to find babysitters and carpool rides for school. I had to accept the vulnerability of my life in making plans for events in the future. Once I was diagnosed with cancer, my life became contingent. I was no longer in control of my future, yet alone daily plans, which were taken up with chemo, radiation, and tests. Such was the case for my caregivers, spouse, and family. All prior family routine stepped aside for the battle—or all-out war—against this illness. I quickly learned to value everyone's personal time within my care network. My children were young and could not fully grasp what was happening. This innocence was probably a benefit, for I could see the fear in their eyes as the treatments killed good cells with the bad. The hair loss was witness to that as an outward and visible declaration. Joe, my husband and partner in life, had to be father, caregiver, and breadwinner all in one, and I couldn't help feeling guilty of the pressure my illness was causing. For the first time in Joe's life, his physician placed him on blood-pressure meds. We had been aware of his family's history of high blood pressure, but it had not surfaced before the stress of my illness. We were both mourning the loss of our freedom to plan on our future together with our children.

Facing the pain in the realization that I might lose my future with my family—knowing I might not see my girls grow up or grow old with my husband—I prepared for this possibility by purchasing a diary for each of my girls. I started the first passage in each with a personal letter sharing my hope that if I should pass they could use the diary to write anything they wanted to share with me. I might not be there physically, but this diary would give them the presence of an object to communicate their feelings through. Later, as they grew older, I presented each one with their diary at the end of their eighth-grade year. As parents of students entering high school, we were asked to write a letter to our children about how important they were to us and our hopes and dreams for their upcoming high-school years. It was a lovely opportunity to share with them the journey we had traveled together. Since I am still here to this day and miracles do happen, I have asked my girls to hold on to their books, not knowing what may be around the corner.

The unending game of diagnostic tests made avoidance possible with its ups and downs. It gave way to hopes built and taken away by poor results in a series of bitter disappointments. Events happen quickly on television medical shows, but not in real life. The victim and our families play the waiting game—waiting on appointments that can't be scheduled soon enough, waiting for test results that can't come quickly enough, waiting for a doctor to call, and hours and days in between. One time a lab forgot to run my biopsy tests before a holiday weekend. When the error was finally addressed after the holiday, I was a basket case. Anger and fear had waged a war inside me during that weekend. I was angry at the incompetence of the lab, the control the test results had on my mental state, and the fear of results that were not what I had hoped for after the unnecessary wait.

If pain is not the result of the disease itself, it is the product of tests and treatments. Cancer is definitely not for the weak-at-heart to endure; when death stared me in the eye, my strength resonated from within. My first exposure to excruciating physical pain came when I awoke in recovery the day of my lymph-node biopsy. The biopsy had been taken just outside my left lung by my heart and proved positive for cancer cells. Prior to the surgery, the doctor explained that if the node tested negative for cancer, the upper left lobe of my lung would be removed. This surgery would involve a lengthy period of time. When I awoke in recovery I looked at the clock. The short lapse of time told the results. Then immediately an extreme pain radiated from my chest as though a knife was still inserted and no amount of pleading with the nurses would help. They kept repeating, "You already received pain meds. We can't give you any more." They thought I was just hysterical from realizing I had cancer.

"Are they nuts? I know the difference between physical and emotional pain!" Luckily the doctor came to my aid, realizing I was one of those unusual patients who did not respond to the particular pain meds I had been prescribed. The nurses quietly avoided eye contact. While dealing with the medical profession, you learn that usually the eyes can tell the story, as emotions are hard to conceal. Being my own advocate, I made sure my choice of pain meds was noted prior to any later surgeries.

Now, many years later, I ventured to my aunt's hope chest to refresh my memory of a story I had heard when I was young. The written document within the Manning Family Tree described the narrative of a soldier ancestor who was bayoneted and left for dead on the battlefield only to survive hours later at an army hospital. I can only envision the true pain he must have felt, not lying as I had in a sterile operating recovery room with doctors and nurses attending to me, but on the bloodstained field amongst the dead, almost forgotten. Stories like these that I have uncovered in my lineage led me to believe that the struggles one faces in battling a disease such as cancer and the importance one places on survival traits and prayer can be what helps one to triumph.

My research into my lineage proved to be something I can look at from a different vantage point now that I've survived. I uncovered an association formed by my cousins, whom I have yet to meet, called the Manning Association. You should Google it; there you will find the words below the family crest, "PER AR-

The Manning family crest

DUA STABILIS," Latin for "Steady over rough ground." So fitting for what I strived for as I battled the disease, and the ground was definitely rough, if not rocky! To look back now at my mother's passing, the family tree, and lineage I was born into, I feel very proud to be a member of this family. We are all survivors, having been born from ancestors who survived so that we could be here today. When one faces death or a disease that can bring about an end to a life as I have, it is common to seek out the meaning in one's existence. Yet in a situation like the death of a parent, you may reach for family ties to link to your life.

After my mother's death, I persuaded my family to take a road trip to the little valley in the Allegheny Mountains called Drury's Run. My mother was born in Drury's Run in 1918 and spent her childhood there. The trip allowed me to relive my childhood visits and gain research on my family through the newspaper archives of the *Renovo Daily Record*. In this small coal-mining town, my maternal grandfather, Harry Batschelet, built his empire from the ground up and was a man admired by friends and family. Looking into the history of the Run, I found that the first cabin was roughly constructed in 1812. The land was used for a saw and "corn cracker" mill. In 1872 Karthus Coal and Lumber Company purchased land in Drury's Run for their lumber and coal company. Even though the company had access to these natural resources, they ran into financial difficulties and were offered for sale. In 1916, my grandfather started Batschelet Mines on land owned by the late James Murphy. He became a well-known coal operator, real-estate investor, and proprietor of the West Branch Hotel and White City Dance Hall. At great expense, he made many extensive improvements to the mines, according to an article on his life in the archives. Among other innovations, he installed an aerial tramway for transporting coal from his mines to the foot of the mountain, quite an accomplishment for the times.

When I first began to consider the possibility of inheriting a personality trait that might have been imprinted on my genes and given me the inborn strength to survive, my grandfather was the first person in my lineage that came to mind. Although I had never met the man, his legacy had made a lasting impression on me since childhood. He was a bigger-than-life hero, with a drive and persistence that created a lucrative and profitable business that supported his family long after his death. He fathered two daughters, Edith and Mary, and then his first wife, Olive, died, leaving the girls motherless and him a widower. After a respectable period of mourning, a young woman, Rhoda Manning, caught Harry's eye. She was from a well-established family who were prominent residents of Liedy Township, according to another article in the *Renovo Daily Record*. Her family dated back to the early settlement of Cambridge.

One early spring day, as the crocuses were beginning to poke their purple heads out of the soil and the sky was yielding a cool April shower, I lit a fire to get the dampness out of the house and sank once again into my cozy chair with the family Bible. With Philomena lounging at my feet, I removed my grandparents' honeymoon picture taken at Niagara Falls, along with their marriage license, dated August 27, 1910. I had to smile at their serious expressions on this typical arcade-quality photograph. Their figures appeared to be cut out and pasted on

Harry & Rhonda Batschelet

a backdrop of the Falls behind them. Rhoda's hair was swept up in a tight, elegant bun from her high, pale forehead, and Harry appeared as though he should be in a barbershop quartet. It's funny how we view ourselves in the present and how we appear to others years down the road into the future.

Setting the Bible down, I picked up the family tree and drifted into the past. In the early colonial times, my grandmother Rhoda's great-grandfather, William Manning, moved to the Bay Colony from England along with his son, William Manning II, to hear the preaching of an English pastor. They both engaged in trade and manufacturing and became men of wealth in Massachusetts. William II and Deacon John Cooper were appointed by the Colonial Government to erect and fund the first permanent brick building of Harvard University, Harvard Hall. William Manning II, like many of our early American settlers, possessed great endurance, making him a survivor in American history. I am proud to be able to trace my roots to such a man.

My lineage continued on through William II to his son, Samuel Manning, and to Billerica, Massachusetts, where in 1696 he erected the Manning Manse, an historical manor house that stands to this day. Samuel's grandson Phineas and his son William joined the same Connecticut regiment when the Revolutionary War broke out and marched up the Hudson River to serve under General Washington. In the fall of 1777 the regiment was ordered to Valley Forge, Pennsylvania, not far from Philadelphia. British sentries spotted the American army and a rear guard was posted to protect the retreat of Lafayette. William was that rear guard. As the British charged, a grenadier's bayonet pierced through his stomach and came out his back. He lay there helpless in the freezing cold for hours until he was transported to Philadelphia. The surgeons told William he owed his life to the fact that he had eaten nothing for three days and the bitterly cold temperatures had helped stop the bleeding. But one cannot keep from wondering what part God and the imprint of personality traits provided the inherent strength he possessed. It was said William lived out his old age showing his grandsons the scars as he told of his service under General Washington.

Samuel Manning's fifth son also carried the name of William. This William witnessed the Battle at Concord and was so moved that he wrote his famous treatise, "The Key of Libberty" in 1798. William was a semiliterate farmer (note his spelling of 'liberty' and the grammatical errors in the following quote from his book) who wrote, "When the war began between Brittan & Amarica I was in the prime of Life & highly taken up with Libberty & a free Government. I See almost the first blood that was shed in Concord fite & scores of men dead, dying, &

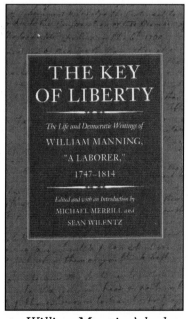

William Manning's book

wounded in the Cause of Libberty, which caused serious sensations in my mind." This excerpt from his book sends chills up my spine; to think that these are the words of a man with whom I share the same lineage. He was greatly affected by the bloodshed, both physically and emotionally, and saw it for what it truly was.

While researching this book one night on the Internet, I came across an article written by Ron Newton, "Rediscovering 'The Key of Liberty' And the Hand That Turns It." I was very excited to find William's book being used in 2010 as a reference and motivational piece for the problems facing our society and government today. I quickly shot Ron Newton an e-mail and learned he has expertise in personality and behavioral traits. Newton's article mentions an historian from Harvard University, Samuel Eliot Morison, who summarized William's determination in the foreword to the 1922 publication of "The Key of Libberty." Morison wrote, "It used to be said of him by his friends that if William Manning were drowned, they would seek his body up-stream, for he surely would not float down with the current like other people!"[2]

This hit home and brought me back forty years to my sixteenth year. When they coined the phrase "Sweet Sixteen," they weren't talking about me—at least in my mother's eyes, William's great-great grandniece. She always made mention of my determination in those teenage years and how it would be the death of me. How wrong she was! I viewed life differently, not like most people. This virtue was my key; it allowed me to be tenacious.

---

2 Manning, William, *The Key of Libberty* [Sic](The Manning Association, Billerica, Massachusetts, 1922) pg. vii.

Some may call it bullheaded; I prefer firm in my convictions. Maybe I inherited that inner self from my ancestors, through my mother or father's lineage, and it made me who I am today.

I read stories like William Manning's at Valley Forge to find a link to my imprint while I pondered the question of inheriting strength from my ancestors. I felt leery of such an undertaking, but asked myself so many questions as a survivor and needed to discover more clues about the sources of my inner strength. How did I find the strength during the private war I waged with my emotions in battling cancer and was it related to the emotional fears my ancestors may have faced throughout the decades? Every bit of information I have found to gain more insight into my inheritance of strength has amazed me. Maybe I also acquired the talent to write and feel the emotions that overtake an individual when faced with the fear of death, as William did that day as he lay helpless on the battlefield in a pool of blood. Well, you can be the judge of that as you are now traveling alongside me in this journey. I hope my research and soul searching is starting to scratch the surface, strengthening you in your quest in life and your imprint.

Fear kills, literally. At this point in my life I can't even

How did I find the strength during the private war I waged with my emotions in battling cancer and was it related to the emotional fears my ancestors may have faced throughout the decades?

let myself say the word; I can't think it. And I can't begin to let it get under my skin. Each day as we battle any sort of struggle, we choose whether to find hope in our faith or to weaken to our fears.

The behavioral traits we may inherit through the power of Selective Adaptation and Epigenetics[3] may come to play in the genes of cancer survivors as our numbers continue to grow. We all need to remind ourselves that we are already survivors, since we are among a part of the human race that has survived long enough to exist.

> *Over thousands of years of evolution, the genes in your body have responded to numerous threats faced by past ancestors and adapted in a way that is useful for survival.*

Over thousands of years of evolution, the genes in your body have responded to numerous threats faced by past ancestors and adapted in a way that is useful for survival. In this our genes have developed abilities and behavioral traits that I believe prompted me to fight rather than flee this disease. With our free will and through our faith in God I truly believe our bodies deserve a fighting chance to survive any battle. You may not win, but then again you might.

---

3 The study of changes in gene expression caused by mechanisms other than changes in the underlying DNA sequence.

4

Facing the Enemy

fter the diagnosis of my first cancer, I became aware of the makings of hospital politics. My attending physicians pleaded my case and the type of treatment I was to receive to the Hospital Tumor Board to no avail. I had never dreamed my life would be held in the balance of an institution's materialistic gains from the awarding of grant monies. A probably selfish motive to the benefit of research, but shouldn't there be an exception to the rule when a prominent doctor pleads for alternative treatment in an unusual case? Especially when the treatment isn't experimental, and the grant is to prove that providing all facets of treatment available— chemo, radiation, and surgery—is not necessary! I had to ask myself, "Where did this grant money come from? Possibly could it have been an insurance company?"

Taking a proactive position against the hospital, my thoracic surgeon contacted an oncologist at a neighboring institution to plan out my treatment. Joe and I would soon learn the value of this new oncologist as a physician and friend. This man had volunteered his time in Calcutta for Mother Theresa and his wife and children volunteer at Hope Clinic International. Upon viewing the peace dove captured in the relief above the main entrance to the cancer wing at this hospital, I knew God's plan had started to unfold for me. The dove is used many times in our religion to represent the Holy Spirit, and I took this as a sign that my spirit was on the right path. This was a time in the battle when I spent all my efforts either directly connected to winning the war for my soul, my life, or my family. My future in this earthly world was contingent on my physical life; I was not sure what this journey to attain survival had in store for me or what would be normal to expect as we entered into a battle in the spring of 1998. Even though I could sense the prognosis, I didn't ask, nor did I want to hear it verbalized. Deep inside me, the spoken word brought about the potential of a sad reality and the possibility that a miracle might not occur. Either because of denial or true faith in the spiritual hereafter, I was drawn both to prayer and the inconceivable inability to admit defeat.

During this time in our struggles, Joe encouraged me to fulfill household responsibilities when I was able, and this helped me keep my respect and worth as a mother, wife, and human being. When I hear someone say to or about a cancer patient that all they have to do is get well, I get angry. To say this puts the responsibility of getting better solely on the victims, while demeaning their value as productive individuals while waging their battles.

Having little time for anything needless or trivial, I devoted my days to lifestyle changes. I learned that if we put anything in or on our bodies that isn't nutritious or organic, our anatomies require energy to digest or dispose of it. This is a great waste of the body's processes when it needs to be harnessing its energy to prevent cancer and other illnesses. Anything that didn't battle cancer or improve health or soul didn't rate on my "to do list."

Previously, I had been a lousy eater who seldom consumed my daily vitamins or the recommended servings of fruit and veggies. I changed my ways to become a proactive organic consumer at the health food stores. I found the owners and employees to be a great resource and a positive addition to my quest, providing uplifting stories of survivors who had fought and beat many diseases. In these establishments you will find survivors and caregivers who have personally witnessed cures and are anxious to give their testimonials. With this you will add new players to your team. I welcomed the assistance of these people with open arms. Very often they had great information and helpful hints.

Each day as we battle any sort of struggle, we choose whether to find hope in our faith or to weaken to our fears.

As I struggled with my disease and treatments, I was forming new friendships and altering my family's lifestyle for the better. I could witness the good results from this battle. I actually felt better on my weeks off chemo than I had felt in years, not only physically but also mentally and spiritually. I had developed a devotion to the Divine Mercy after viewing a movie on St. Faustina's life and I tried to spread the word of what it was achieving for me in my heart and soul. A trust in a positive outcome of my battle brought with it a comfort that whatever result occurred, I was on the right path in this journey.

The effects of the chemo brought sleepless nights of aching joints as my body responded to the poison circulating in my veins. My mind rushed aimlessly, hoping for the Adivan to kick in and overtake the anxiety. It was on one of those countless nights as my family slept that I found myself in prayer and conversation with the Lord. On one night in particular I had been soaking in a hot bath to get some sort of relief. I made a promise to Jesus that should He find it within His will to spare my life, I would devote that life He had given me in dedication to spreading the devotion to "The Divine Mercy." In keeping with my promise, I sought from Him a favor that I would never forget my pledge. Through this conversation and the events of the next two cancers, I reminded my soul of its devotion to bring souls the Chaplet, the key to unlocking eternal life. It was in the events within my battles that I began to see our Lord's word landing on

Jesus, I trust in You

Hyla Image of The Divine Mercy

© 1992 Congregation of the Marians of the Immaculate Conception, Stockbridge, MA 01263. All Rights Reserved. Reprinted with permission.

otherwise deaf ears and flourishing in souls through my cancer journeys and my cures.

Since the year 2000, the Catholic faith has recognized St. Faustina and Divine Mercy Sunday, to which Jesus has made a promise of intercession at the hour of death to those believers who follow His word and trust in Him. These words were of great comfort to me during my battle.

Image of Saint Maria Faustina Kowalska based on her Passport photo

© Congregation of the Marians of the Immaculate Conception, Stockbridge, MA 01263. All Rights Reserved. Reprinted with permission.

The devotion gave me strength to hold on should I not survive and a purpose to my suffering with a further path to follow should I survive. The documented history shows that Jesus appeared to Faustina, a young Polish nun, prior to WWII. Through her visions, He asked her to bring souls to Him through the prayers of the Chaplet. These prayers can be said on rosary beads. There is a painting of His image as He appeared to St. Faustina inscribed with the words, "Jesus I trust in You."

After only two treatments of chemo used in battling non-small cell lung cancer, a CT showed that a possible miracle had occurred in my chest; the cancer could not be seen. Only surgery would substantiate its disappearance. I was praying the "Divine Mercy Chaplet" on the first Friday in July 1998, at 3:10 p.m. with my youngest daughter Frannie on my lap when the call with the results came. Cast as a heroine in this Cancer Epic, I realized for the first time the melodramatic role I played and the urgent need I had to share my journey of experiences.

After the surgery to remove and biopsy the upper lobe of my left lung, the pain medication made it impossible for me to concentrate on my readings or prayer. Drifting in and out of short catnaps, I listened to the Irish melodies Joe had gotten for me and packed in my hospital bag. I found a peaceful place for my thoughts to travel and connect with my roots. Maybe it was an innate link to my heritage that brought me home to souls from my family long gone; perhaps it was their blood that flowed through my veins in an epigenetic voyage of the genes that I didn't recognize at that time.

As I recovered from surgery, the biopsy results supported the fact that the miracle I had prayed for had been granted, and I underwent radiation as an added insurance policy against reoccurrence. In the department of radiology I prepared for the making of a plaster cast of my upper torso. The treatment would mean daily doses of x-rays. This involved lying motionless on my back while a precise beam would assault the area inside and outside my lung where cancer cells might still be hiding. To insure the beam was focused correctly I was introduced to the world of body tattoos. Small black dots were placed on my serum and rib cage, another source of permanent reminders of my battle with cancer that I bear to this day.

For the next few weeks, my friends took turns accompanying me to the hospital for these treatments. I learned a lot about my friends during those weeks. I was very grateful to all those who helped our family; they showed what it truly means to be Christian in helping their neighbor. It takes stepping outside your comfort zone to help and not try to live in a picture-perfect world for the sheer sake of remaining selfishly comfortable.

While I lay still on the table as though on a tanning bed, I was quite aware that I wasn't preparing for a trip to the beach, but I could daydream of a Caribbean vacation just the same. Mostly, I prayed for the beam to seek out and attack any cells running around in my chest, as though I was playing Laser Tag. In the last few weeks of treatment and a number of weeks thereafter my skin showed the burning effects of radiation, but the worst was the burn inside on my esophagus, which made even swallowing my own spit hurt. I can only describe the pain as one I might have felt while learning the craft of a fire-eater in a circus and failing miserably. My treatments ended Halloween Day and as the burning increased I was propelled by an invisible warrior inside me unable to give up his battle. By Thanksgiving, with fuzz appearing on my head, I looked like a true soldier sporting a buzz cut. We decided to travel to Frankenmuth, a small German town, to celebrate the holiday and give the family a break from a life revolving around cancer. It was enjoyable for everyone except me when it came to eating the three main entrees of turkey, chicken, and duck. But I was alive, so I counted my blessings in the squash, applesauce, and ice cream, hoping the Christmas ham would be more palatable.

My memory of the disease and treatments were put into perspective by their uncanny ability to appear and disappear during holiday seasons, or maybe it was the effect they had on my family at special times in my children's lives. Anyway, my memory of the treatment for my first cancer coincided with the Easter holidays of 1998.

My first battle was probably the scariest of all. Once I reached the ten-year mark, I bravely summoned the courage to ask my doctor what my chances had been in the beginning. I learned that I had only had a 15% or lower chance of surviving back in 1998. Having learned this ten years later, I always tell cancer victims to not seek out the prognosis. It served me no purpose and could have discouraged my battle. The miraculous disappearance of my enemy after only two chemo treatments didn't fit the gloomy prognosis I had initially faced for a stage-three lung-cancer patient. Of course, that is the essence of this book, and why I have chosen to share the search and journey I traveled to be here today. I choose to look toward the positive to where miracles can and do happen. For this reason, no patient should be put in the position to talk about his or her body as if it is detached from its soul. I am eternally grateful in this respect to my oncologist. Most medical professionals handle critical illness by detaching from their patients, probably a mental tactic to minimize the emotions that might cause them pain. Whatever the reason, most physicians respond in a cool and professional manner, laying out a plan of attack for the enemy, the illness. Depending on his or her position as general in this battle, the physician may or may not accept the patient as an active participant.

Most physicians will usually act as they have been trained. They will not express that they recognize the fear and frustration that goes along with disease. I have to count my blessings once again to be under the care of a wonderful Christian oncologist, who is gifted not only in knowledge of cancer, but in the ability to handle the psychological needs of his patients. I can only guess the daily stress this man handles with cancer patients. I will always be grateful for the time he took when I needed it. Even though I had to wait many times past my appointment times to see him, I knew the reason for this was that his patients came first, not the ticking of the clock, and I was not just a patient, but a person. When I reached the point of remission with my first cancer, he took on an intern who was also a survivor. What a blessing! This woman was so affected by her experience with the disease that she dedicated her career to battling the illness. Her shared insight about the unending emotional torture of the wait time between medical testing and receiving the results was invaluable. She gave me suggestions that eased my fear—a fear that made me feel like a terrified field mouse waiting for the pounce from the ferocious cat crouched in hiding, always wondering if I could outrun or outsmart my attacker. The medical field truly needs to see the value that survivors can play in the caring and recovery periods of cancer patients. It is that old adage "been there, done that," that means so much. This was another step in experiences that I was graced with, as though God had me by the hand, helping me down the path, and was waiting at every bend in the road. At the time, I didn't see it, but now as I write this book the vision is clear.

I had undiscovered places inside me that hungered for knowledge buried deep within my soul—a kind of world I knew not. The worst of it is that I woke up from my present world facing my previous life of surface gratification and the guilt that came with it. I was unsure about asking for the desires that were buried deep inside me and for what I was facing in the remission to come. Driven by the strength in my trust that I had survived and weakened by the self-destructive feeling that comes from the unknown, my every thought was driven to reach out to the rays of hope streaming from Jesus' heart. I came to this moment in time seeking to be nurtured and found what fit naturally in my life of prayer, "The Chaplet of Divine Mercy."

Sharing this illness with someone you truly care about—be it a spouse, a child, a parent, a family member, or a close friend—allows you to be graced with the true meaning of life.

Individuals never look good in their darkest hour. Yet it's those hours that can make us who we are. We can stand strong and emerge victorious. I had reached my comfort zone in a mental state where I found trust. In that trust somewhere deep inside me, I knew beyond a doubt the existence of something greater, wiser, and unconditionally more loving than I.

We each face many challenges in our individual lives, and for a cancer victim the challenges are even greater. Sharing this illness with someone you truly care about—be it a spouse, a child, a parent, a family member, or a close friend—allows you to be graced with the true meaning of life. I sometimes ponder over those souls who avoid the challenges in life they find unpleasant. Do they not realize that someday, unless they die in an accident, they will face a serious illness? When I found myself pitying my children and the struggles they faced with my illness, I told myself that at least they learned a valuable lifelong lesson firsthand in how to face a critical illness or serious physical disability.

While battling a deadly disease, I became aware of the different reactions people exhibited toward me. Some would feel such pity that they couldn't do enough, while others strangely exhibited feelings of guilt, possibly from being spared the disease that befell my body. Others were just curious or tried to distance themselves from the uncomfortable situation they did not understand and were unable to deal with. I offer to you: Do not, under any circumstances, take the reactions of others to heart. Instead, offer prayers for them during their limited existence. Remain filled with grace and feel blessed to journey through this battle holding your head high. Hopefully through example you will eliminate some of this ignorance.

My children also witnessed the value and true meaning behind "for better or worse" and "in sickness and health." The love between a husband and wife can be a great challenge. Facing a battle with a spouse's critical illness is even greater. You can use this time to strengthen and build on your relationship. Not facing this experience together would discount the value of your time spent thus far in your marriage.

It is human to feel left behind when someone's life makes a change from what you have grown accustomed to. The same can happen when you are stricken with cancer. Not wanting to trade places with anyone battling a critical disease, family members—especially caregivers and children of the victim—face an inner conflict as their lives change due to the circumstances. They may have to face feelings of jealousy as the victim appears to be receiving all the attention. With children, Mom or Dad's attention may be fixed on the battle and less on them.

I don't like to admit it, but I found some of my friends and family members reacted to my illness with denial. They were afraid to truly look into my eyes and accept my disease. It was as if it were contagious or that accepting it made them face the reality that it could happen to them. It made me sad to feel the avoidance emanating from them. These individuals tried to paint a fairy-tale life for themselves, one that was devoid of anything ugly or unpleasant. It was a life that had no place for the reality of cancer. To even acknowledge that I might not survive caused them to flee from their involvement in my journey. It is for these souls I now pray.

During my mother's last years, I realized for the first time that some people view seniors with the same special invisibility that they offer cancer patients. It's as if by not acknowledging the elderly, they can ignore the same aging process in themselves that is visibly appearing with each tick of the clock. Sad as it is, I so often think of these people when I see souls missing out on the true meaning of such a gift as a life.

5

Those Who Came Before

s a child and again as a cancer victim, I fondly remembered my paternal grandmother's devotion to daily rosaries. I recently gave my youngest daughter the small child's rosary my grandmother presented my father on the day of his Holy Communion. That moment brought back memories of years ago when I had more diligently said my daily rosary in the long stressful months filled with chemo and radiation treatments. My spirit had been strengthened by the power of the Blessed Virgin and my soul imprinted with the fight for survival. We measure our lives sometimes not with hours, days, months, or even years, but in those special times in our lives that we share with those we love. There is a feeling of oneness with God when you find the path you need to follow. This occurred a few times during my journey, and never was it more frequent as when I prayed daily. This devotion to daily prayers, rosary, and chaplet gave me a time to meditate on my experiences and seek peace in my soul as I sought to heal not only physically and psychologically but also spiritually.

This was also the case for Bridget and Hamilton, my paternal grandparents, at the Easter Vigil on the sixteenth of April in the year 1911. After they made personal sacrifices during the Lenten season, Hamilton entered into the Roman Catholic faith in a quaint little church in England. They had been apart for the long winter as Bridget's work as a household servant required her to spend the cold months in London with the royal family, while Hamilton worked in the damp shipyards of the Isle of Wight.

As I now sit at my favorite table in the corner of the local coffee shop, Al is brewing up an espresso for one of his regular customers, a very nice Italian man, who has recommended a must-see chapel carved into the side of a mountain on Italy's western coast line if Joe and I are lucky enough to travel again to Europe. Leaning over, I extract my father's large manila envelope from my book bag to study the contents. Upon bending back the metal clasp that is holding the envelope's flap shut, I peer inside to see a familiar face looking back at me. Though years younger than I remember and sitting for a portrait with other household servants of the royal family, there is my paternal grandmother.

Bridget Theresa Gaffney was born poor in the small rural village of Drumconrath, County Meath, Ireland, on January twelfth, 1882 with genes that gave her strength and stamina. Born with the dark hair and clear blue eyes that can be traced through her bloodline to Spanish or Algerian pirates and termed "Black Irish," she grew up in a small cottage of turf sod with thatched roof lacking the luxury of running water. A cross of St. Bridget, the mother of Ireland, hung in the roof beams protecting their little cottage from sparks 'comin' out thee chimney,' as she would have phrased it. "He made the Father, the Son, and the Holy Spirit, but the Irish made the Mother," Grandmother would say. Many an Irishman would think of the saint as the Mary of Ireland, so pure and gentle. Set in forested drumlin countryside, Meath is surrounded by vast lakes and mountains. Folklore tells of a dragon roaming in the deep waters of Lough Braken Lake and the dense forests of Drumconrath. The dragon was said to hold the key to becoming a true Irishman. The legend tells of a strong noble tribe from ancient Druminshin who entered the dragon's lair and slayed the beast. Thus the villagers became known as the True Men of Ireland. Bridget knew little of what lay beyond the natural boundaries of the village. Life was poor but simple for her Irish family who worked the land with callused hands and sweat pooling on their brows. They survived with a natural strength and a strong faith in God. They suffered thru the famine by living for their dreams.

The term "Black Irish" is believed by some geneticists to be linked to the Irish Y chromosomes. Agricultural societies such as Bridget's worked the land and my grandfather Steen's family toiled as ironworkers in the shipyards of the British Isles. Historians of the Icelandic population believe that this part of the world originated in the Viking and Celtic nationalities. This theory merges the personality trait of heroism of the Norse and the cultural traditions possessed by the Celtic people. Historians look upon a study of the human genome as a rich source of information.

Bridget's immediate ancestors lived through the Potato Famine that besieged Ireland. As mentioned in Chapter One, the theory of epigenetics strongly points to the possibly of developing epigenetic imprints that are, more than likely, passed down. Evidence supports a variety of psychologists' claims suggesting that personality traits, temperament, and intelligence can be affected by epigenetic inheritance. In researching selective adaptation, I uncovered that genes for traits most useful in survival can show an increase in frequency, thus making it more likely for the bearer of such genes to survive. Related to evolution and if you can excuse the cliché, to "Survival of the Fittest," this theory suggests that the incredible fortitude Bridget's ancestors showed to survive the famine was imprinted into her genetic code.

My own journey has created awareness within myself of the many roads a cancer victim can follow in managing and recovering that period in his or her life during and following treatment. I have realized the importance of the ups and downs of the diagnostic journey, the acceptance journey, the treatment journey, and the recovery journey. All my experiences through this illness served the purpose of making me the person I am today. Hopefully I'm better for it, if not more understanding.

Sometime in the year 1901, searching for a better life and struggling to survive on her own, Bridget traveled a winding country road with only a few items of clothing slung over her shoulder in a worn garment bag. She found temporary employment for a short time in Dublin on the way to the neighboring County Kildara. There, at the end of her journey, she earned work as a cook at Curragh

Camp, a military camp for the British. Though she was only seventeen, Bridget's homestyle farm cooking drew the attention of the hungry young soldiers. It wasn't long before Duke Arthur, the son of Queen Victoria, and his wife, the Duchess of Connaught, also residing at the camp, heard of the new cook's culinary skills. The Duke and Duchess needed service for their three young sons and daughter, so Bridget joined their household.

Bridget Theresa Gaffney

Bridget was a much-welcomed asset to Prince Arthur of Battenburg and his family. Her devout religious background and strong family values contrasted to the manly goings-on at the camp, which had a reputation that left much to be desired. Queen Victoria had spent four decades agonizing over the misdeeds of Arthur's eldest brother Edward VII, and his episode with a young woman, Nellie Clifden. He had been in training at the camp for his future role as King and head of Britain's Armed Forces. His behavior very well may have aided in the death of his father. Prince Albert, unaware of his poor health due to contracting typhoid, ventured to meet with the young prince to express his disappointment in the youth's actions. Upon returning to Windsor, Albert, the prince consort, died.

Four years passed at the camp, and in 1905 Bridget was moved to a new household within the royal family, that of Princess Beatrice, the youngest of Queen Victoria's children and sister to Prince Arthur. It is said that because Beatrice's daughter Ena was engaged to King Alfonso of Spain, she needed a household servant who could instruct her in the Catholic faith. This union required the young princess to renounce her faith in the Church of England and her succession to the English throne. Mary, the wife of the Prince of Wales, wrote Princess Beatrice on the day of Ena's reception into the Catholic Church conducted by Monsignor Brindle, the Catholic Bishop of Nottingham. The letter advised the princess to keep Ena somewhere at Osborne Cottage on the Isle of Wight as there was turmoil in London over her conversion.

It was during this time in Beatrice's household that Bridget helped the young princess Ena prepare for her life as a Catholic and for her wedding-day Mass. This tidbit was noted in a letter to my father from his sister. Also enclosed was a photograph of the princess signed and dated, which had been in my grandmother's possession when she died. The history books stated that the union of Ena and Alfonso started as a fairytale wedding on May 31st, 1906. Princess Beatrice presented her daughter with gifts of exquisite lace, diamond jewelry, pink pearls, hair ornaments, and a stained-wood inlaid jewel case. King Edward and Queen Alexandra presented their niece a parure of diamonds and oblong turquoises.

In keeping with the Spanish custom, the king gave his future queen her crown of jewels and a white wedding dress embroidered in silver. Alfonso positioned a guard in place during the night to protect his bride. The following day, as the ceremony neared the end of a long procession-al, an anarchist, Mateo Morral, threw a bomb disguised as a bouquet of flowers as the newlyweds passed below the balcony on which he stood. They escaped unharmed, though the new queen's gown was splattered with blood. Horses, soldiers, and an outrider were killed and many were injured. The fairytale turned deadly, but the royals showed much courage.

When you are seriously sick, you may fall weak to pity parties and question why this illness is happening to you. As you spend hours watching television or DVDs while resting from treatments, you may wonder why your life has been so hard, especially when you see beautiful people on the screen living such glamorous lives. Such may have been the case watching the recent wedding of Prince William and Princess Kate. You may have wondered what a royal life would be like. While it may look as though roy-als live in a fantasyland where all their desires come true, it is not always the case, such as on Princess Ena's wed-ding day. She also endured her first baby being born a hemophiliac. In subsequent years, her fourth baby died within her womb near the end of her pregnancy as her husband distanced himself from the relationship. Dur-ing May 1910, Princess Beatrice not only lost her brother, King Edward, but a grandson she was never able to hold. At this time, Osborne Cottage and all the houses of the royal family felt the weight of the losses they faced.

Henry Steen

Osborne House sat on the small Isle of Wight in the English Channel where the royals traditionally summered. Queen Victoria built Osborne House, and Beatrice received Osborne Cottage as her summer home upon Victoria's death. The Isle is also known for its military services and shipbuilding. It was here that my great grandfather, Henry Steen, under orders of Her Royal Highness' Military, was relocated. Henry was a military man who fought in the Boer War and served in India for Her Majesty's Empire as a member of the Sea Forth Highlanders in the Scottish Infantry of the British Army. He had previously lived in Northeast Scotland in Wick Caithness on Bridge Street. My grandfather Hamilton was born there on April 13, 1887. Their clan started in Caithness from Norman origins in the 1400s. William the Conqueror, the founder of the Clan of Sinclair, was an ancestor possessing great strength. His stronghold was located at Roslin Castle even after the clan became Earls of Orkney on the Caithness mainland. It is easy to find a DNA connection to survival in men such as these.

Wick, Caithness lays at the mouth of the Wick Bay opening into the North Sea. This region is known for its shipbuilding and its harbor. The Steen family came from a long line of shipbuilders who spoke Scottish Gaelic, the customary language in Wick. This Celtic language is native to Scotland and descended from the primitive Irish Language.

As a young boy, Hamilton sang in the choir at the First Church of St. James. Hamilton especially enjoyed Sundays in the summer when Princess Beatrice, a member of the parish, would attend. The mother church of St. James was at Whippingham on the Isle, the burial site of both the princess' father and husband. So devoted was her faith that Beatrice graced the chapel with her engagement rings, which were affixed to the chalice stem. The satin from her wedding dress skirted the altar.

Like Beatrice, my grandmother held a strong conviction of the value of our faith in survival. Struggles can either strengthen your beliefs or threaten them. Many a "chosen one"—as I like to call those of us who have battled or are battling a life-threatening illness—have found an answer in God. In this answer I uncovered the important message of discovering what this illness provided for me, not what it took away. As I journeyed through my treatments and survived this adventure, I gained strength and the ability

Tradition is the chain we hold on to from one generation to the next. You may not be remembered in generations to come but tradition may go on—in it we will be remembered—one link at a time.

to reconnect with others and myself. A friend who fought kidney disease for a lifetime once told me of his own poor

health, "We are the lucky few, for we can see our vulnerability and take what time we have now to make changes
to our lives. Many in today's society of greedy material-
ism and abundant sexual temptations settle for the devil's
treasures and tomorrow may never come for them as they
step off the curb, sit behind that driver's wheel, board a
plane, not to mention all the dangers faced by terrorism,
war, and natural disasters. We have been given a grace;
don't waste it. See it for what it is and feel blessed."

Most young boys in Britain like my grandfather loved
a good game of football, a sport we Americans have re-
named soccer. In this sport Hamilton was given a grace
excelling beyond most of his friends. Slight of build and
quick as a hiccup, he was invited to join the East Cowes
Victoria Football Club. The club is the longest registered
in the English Football Association. The East Cowes Victoria Football Club, or the Vics, derived their name from
the fact that their home field is on Beatrice Avenue. The
avenue was part of the crown estate and owned by Osborne House, the home of the late Queen Victoria and
Prince Consort Albert. In 1889 the Isle of Wight Football Association introduced cup competitions. The trophy was made of solid gold and reported to be the most
valuable football trophy in the world. In 1907, on home
ground, with Princess Beatrice and a few of her household
in attendance, my grandfather, as captain, led his team to
victory. In the presence of royalty on the crown estate, the
Vics won the Gold Cup.

This trophy was reportedly locked in a bank and insured
for the night of presentation. Following the ceremony, the
trophy was returned to the bank's safe. To this day, over

120 years later, I have memories of passing this photo at my grandparents' rented duplex. The photograph depicted my grandfather in uniform front and center with the Gold Cup just to his right and his teammates surrounding him. I can only imagine the pride and honor he must have felt.

When remission arrives, think of it as the Gold Cup, your trophy for a battle well fought. Do not let this time in your life as a survivor pass you by only to be shoved into the back of your mind, as that old pair of socks in your dresser drawer. Even though memories can be painful—when you come to the end—remember that's where the life God has given you begins. A journey to any religious belief, as in remission, isn't without bumps and most of all it isn't usually logical. To face our fate without faith is a lonely place.

Hamilton is in the center row to the right of the Gold Cup

All too many humans who find their prayers unanswered or witness good people stricken by a critical illness resort to blaming God. Actually, it is more advantageous to think God listened and decided that what you asked for is not of His will, than to not have a God to ask. For myself, I tried to begin each day of my illness looking for ways to use my challenges to touch another soul in a positive manner. This gave meaning to each day of my journey and my life. As a noble solider, I faced each day going into battle, fighting for a greater cause—at the hospital chemo clinic, the grocery store, taking a walk down Main Street in our small Midwest town, or any place I could make a connection with another human being. Retreating to my bed at night to say my nightly prayers, I would play back the day, searching for a soul I might have touched as a result of the road I traveled. Better to witness all there is to witness and experience all there is to experience than to not have a life at all. I strove to be more like St. Faustina in the days I had.

There are many things that are essential to arriving at true peace of mind, and one of the most important is faith, which cannot be acquired without prayer.
—John Wooden

6

A Bad Hair Day

September 2000

hen my mother was eleven, both her parents died only days apart. They left seven children to be raised by her oldest sibling, Amy, who was a mere eighteen years old. This emotionally significant event in my mother's early childhood led to a phobia I personally witnessed in following years. Afraid of any impending peril I might encounter, unknowingly she created in me a fear of being on my own or in any questionable position that might risk even the slightest danger. I now find myself having to resist the same urge to overprotect my girls. Luckily Joe is aware of these inner fears after witnessing their inhibiting effects on my life. He reminds me not to be as overprotective with our girls. Mother was so afraid of any threat that her over protectiveness created doubts still chained to me to this day, not to mention the epigenetic marks or imprint I hold within my physical and psychological being.

During my first cancer in 1998, after my surgery and treatments, I fell into a depressed state. Technically I was cured. The surgery showed no evidence of cancer and the follow-up treatments of chemo and radiation served as an insurance policy against any recurrence of

We are the lucky few, for we can see our vulnerability and take what time we have now to make changes to our lives.

the disease. I was still depressed even though I had made it against all odds. Evidently this is common in survivors; when all the adrenalin subsides and the treatment ends, there is sadness. Survivors can have a hard readjustment period trying to get back to a normal way of life. Overtaken by compulsive cleanliness in an effort to control my environment, I developed an obsession with having my house clean and in perfect order. My counselor said it was my way of dealing with what had happened. Since I could not control everything in my life—such as contracting cancer again—it was my way of controlling what I could inside the walls of my home. But my home also held three teenage daughters. Those of you raising children know is impossible to keep a tidy house without going completely nuts in an unmerciful environment. To my kids, I am totally sorry for all the ranting and raving about clothes on the floor, beds unmade, and make-up and hair products everywhere. I thank the dear Lord every day for the gift to share in these moments, as messy as they can be.

To those of you who may be survivors of whatever you have endured, do not fail to realize that the same strength used to battle the situation can grace you with the ability to value your life. You now have the opportunity to make the changes creating the new person whom you as a survivor must get to know. You will never be that same person, so embrace it and treat it as a gift. Share it with others as I now share myself with you.

Throughout my years and experiences with cancer, I found numerous unanswered questions, as is the case with any disease the medical field tries to solve. It is not a science of one-way paths or certainty. There are variables to every case because we are humans created by our Lord and not manmade creatures. To seek out an answer may have no purpose, as the true purpose is finding yourself in this journey.

Two years into my lung cancer remission, by second battle began. I was to return to my old feeling of gut-turning nausea as life and death collided in my inner being. The day had started out with great promise as I dropped my youngest off for her first full day in kindergarten and was reminded by my oldest daughter that I had promised to take her shopping for her first bra after school. As I watched my daughters enter the school building that warm September morning, there was a crispness in the air and the smell of autumn days approaching. It was a day I had dreamed I would be able to witness two years prior when my prognosis was bleak. I headed to my Mothers' Bible Study, the first for the school year, held every Tuesday morning after school Mass in our Catholic Church and school community. The study was made up of school moms who had been a great support to me in the previous two years of battling lung cancer and throughout my remission. I drew tremendous strength from this church community, knowing that each time I went in for surgery or treatment I was included in their prayers. One's prayers strengthen your soul but the prayers of others, especially children, are heaven sent when you are on an operating table. During my illness, my mother-in-law shared with me the graces one can gain in a child's prayer. Each time I was wheeled into the operating room her words came back to me; I knew my children were adding their mother to the list of intentions in their morning prayers. I cannot explain to you what it is like knowing you are prayed for when you are about to drift off into oblivion on that steel table other than to say it is like each prayer is a soul holding your hand.

At the end of our Bible Study, I dreaded going for my yearly checkup and not being able to enjoy our weekly luncheon with the other moms. I entered the ramp to the highway having no fear that this mammogram would be any different than my previous tests. I had no family history of breast cancer, and looking at the odds, I said to myself, "No one gets lung cancer and then becomes stricken with breast cancer two years later." Non-small cell lung cancer doesn't travel to the breast, though the reverse is true and breast cancer can travel to the lungs. My research on the disease had taught me enough to know that fact. Yet an hour later I was in tears, not wanting to accept what I was being told. My favorite intern at the oncologist's office was there to answer my call and the array of questions I had. Later that evening my dear oncologist made time to call after his last patient. This connection alone gave me strength in the knowledge my doctors were aware of my plight and there to help along the way should a biopsy prove needed.

Returning to the car pool pickup line after school, I did my best to conceal from the girls what my heart and soul was going through, and we went shopping. Since Joe was out of town on business, we also went to our favorite diner. As I lay in bed that night saying my prayers, the phone rang. The tears fell as I told my husband the news. His never-ending optimism was present as always. God had graced me with the husband I needed.

Risks in treatment choices are inevitable and this was the case when I was to start an aggressive and optional chemo treatment. My oncologist sat both Joe and I down and opened up his heart to us like no other medical profes-

Do not, under any circumstances, take the reactions of others to heart.

sional had up to this point. We were about to walk over to the part of the cancer wing to start my first infusion after my appointment. This man is a human being first and foremost, and we had come to gratefully respect him for his sensitivity and knowledge of the physical and emotional needs of his cancer patients. In my thirteen years as his patient, I've learned that my oncologist is a man of strong faith whom I truly believe is not only a man of medicine, but also one of God's gifts to mankind.

He confided in us that he had spent much time praying and soul searching as to the best treatment for my cancer. We gratefully appreciated his candor while making this treatment choice. Choices are one of the inevitable circumstances cancer patients and anyone who is terminally ill must face. After all, it is your body and your life. To think that this Christian doctor had actually taken the time to pray over my case gave Joe and me the additional strength we needed to make a decision to advance forward on this battlefield.

As I searched for answers to this new cancer, the doctors also searched by ordering lengthy genetic surveys. They hypothesized that the origin was from radiation exposure during my teenage years as doctors monitored a spinal scoliosis condition. Now twenty-five years later,

Caregivers who ask patients what they need will not always receive a coherent answer. As a result, many victims haven't found and may never find a true source of comfort.

my body was producing primary cancers in my chest. To think that trying to correct one medical problem could cause another was bad enough, but to add insult to injury, my scoliosis was not a critical illness and one I could have lived with. The final blow came from the knowledge that the curve of my spine was now much worse than it had been many years before and the monitoring of the brace with all its x-rays had not even worked!

Traveling forward on my journey through the decision to go ahead with the planned chemo treatments, I suffered the inevitable reaction my body faced having this poison flow through my veins. For each female cancer patient dealing with chemo, there comes the moment in time—vain as it may be—to deal with the effects on the hair. Mine came as I was standing in my shower one morning a few weeks after receiving my first treatment and felt the water rising up over the top of my feet. Looking down in amazement, I saw there was a huge clump of hair swirling around and clogging drain. Stepping out, I gently patted my remaining hair dry and called my friend to enlist her help as I couldn't stop shaking. I knew this day was coming, as it had with my first cancer, but the reality of it had never really hit home. We packed the kids in her minivan and off we went to the wig salon in the mall. I'm sure when we entered the shop with five little girls in tow the sales clerk probably thought, "Here comes trouble."

I quickly spotted a cute, sassy brunette wig above my reach. I asked, "Can I try on that wig on the top shelf?"

The saleswoman curtly answered, "I'm sorry, we only let customers who really need wigs try them on."

Caught off-guard by this reply, I reached up to my hair, which was just waiting for the slightest breeze to leave me, and grabbed a handful. My girls' mouths dropped and their eyes bugged out as they stared at their crazy mother with a bald spot on top of her head.

"Well, I think I qualify, don't you?" I expounded with my hair in my hand.

It was one of those priceless moments we still laugh about to this day. I can picture in my memory the saleswoman turning three shades of red and hurriedly ascending her stepladder getting the wig down for me. Her efforts were not in vain; I purchased the wig and it was always my favorite throughout all my treatments. I bought a new wig for each time I was diagnosed, yet always gravitated back to this one at some point. My purchases of a new wig was a way of treating myself, trying on blonde

Playing dress up

to jet black, short and spiky to long and curly and everywhere in between. In five years I alternated from being a short dark brunette to being a medium-length ash
brown and then topping it off with a curly redhead style.
I bought an assortment of hats and scarves, having fun
with my newfound baldness. My daughters and I would
play dress up. Each of us took turns trying on different
wigs or hats and taking pictures of each other. It was a
great stress reliever, and laughing is the best medicine for
the soul. Then out of the mouth of babes... One day my

daughter requested that I not change my hairstyle quite so frequently. I guess I was having too much fun and the kids at school were starting to place bets on what I would have on my head at carpool time!

The hospital where I received my treatments was wonderful. They had a program funded by well-known cosmetic companies and a very kind and talented cosmetologist who took her time to show us ways to apply eyeliner to make it appear like we had eyelashes and eyebrows. When you lose your hair you lose it everywhere! Yep, even there! So throw away your razors, girls. It's one of those unspoken benefits of chemo.

"Through humor, you can soften some of the worst blows that life delivers. And once you find laughter, no matter how painful your situation might be, you can survive it."

—Bill Cosby

Like most other victims of a life-threatening illness, I questioned my faith and myself, looking at the test results in disbelief and finding a world that appeared surreal. As the fog cleared, my anxiety escalated, and I spent hours searching for answers, cures, and hope. The hope came to me in the form of a Bible verse. I followed my shepherd, Jesus, through the gate as in John 10: 1-10, relying on my faith to give me the strength to fight for my survival. I was defiantly imprinted with what my husband likes to call a significant emotional event, one that was life changing, as it brought with it the ability to study my being from an entirely different perspective. It is in this moment of my journey that I found the importance of resisting the temptation to curl up into a cocoon and hibernate until spring. I became keenly aware that I would not wake up and find this to be a bad dream. In the realization of this reality I was the victim panicking in my own way. To liken it to a stage demeans it. Knowing that other victims have the same feelings may help, but it may also make the fear and disorientation impersonal. The normality of these feelings does not dissolve them. Only time will help the victim to understand what he or she needs. Caregivers who ask patients what they need will not always receive a coherent answer. As a result, many victims haven't found and may never find a true source of comfort.

I found my source of comfort in The Chaplet of Divine Mercy. In a vision to St. Maria Faustina Kowalska in 1935, Jesus revealed a powerful prayer. To this prayer he promised extraordinary graces. St. Faustina recorded in her diary her visions of our Lord. In the dairy it is said, "Through the chaplet you will obtain everything, if what you ask for is compatible with My will (1731)(2)[4]. Through the promises of Our Lord and the strength I was graced, I survived. It is in this faith I still am blessed. There is much to be learned from our inner being and soul, as you will continue to see throughout this book.

My illness caused me to wage an inner battle, not only against my cancer but also against how my path

---

4 Diary: St. Maria Faustina Kowalska, *Divine Mercy in My Soul* (Congregation of Marians of the Immaculate Conception, Stockbridge, MA 012363, 1987) (1731)

to survival came about. Was this grace given to me by the Almighty as a blessing in and of itself? Or was it the result of the free will he has bestowed on me as seen in the sins of our forefathers? Had I used my will and determination inherited through an epigenetic imprint to survive, thus using His graces to their fullest capabilities? Whatever the answer is, I am eternally grateful for my experiences, which have allowed me to witness the unconditional help I received from my family and friends during this time. I experienced and continue to experience benefits within the losses.

You will mourn, as I did, a loss of your freedom to plan on a future with your children. With each consecutive cancer this freedom was chipped away further as I wondered if my battle would ever come to an end.

As the victim of a deadly disease you need to become your own advocate. At the time of my diagnosis, my husband Joe expressed his affection through tough love and prayer and lots of it. The tough love got me so mad that I channeled my anger into a war against the disease. His actions caused my reactions, as I asked myself why he was so determined to have me doing so much work around the house since he had hired a woman to help with some of the household duties. He told her not to cook meals or to do anything he felt I could

I am eternally grateful for my experiences, which have allowed me to witness the unconditional help I received from my family and friends during this time.

physically handle for the kids or myself. I felt this was an open invitation for the new housekeeper to slack off, so I ended up resenting this stranger's presence in my home collecting a paycheck. I was determined to prove to Joe that our money would be better spent on vitamins and good wholesome organic products. My stubbornness actually gave me a good measure of determination to battle this disease. Once again, I recognized my ancestor William Manning and how his body would not float downstream with the current.[5] Stubbornness can be good or bad depending on your situation.

---

[5] Morison, Samuel Eliot, Foreword, *The Key of Libberty* [Sic] (The Manning Association, Billerica, Massachusetts, 1922).

7

Situations in Life

n 1918, my grandparents, Bridget and Hamilton, had been separated due to World War I. Bridget was alone with two young children in London as she remained under employment to the royal household of Princess Beatrice. It was just before Beatrice's grandniece, the sixth child of her sister Alice, Alexandra Tsarina of Russia, along with Beatrice's five great-grandnieces and nephews were executed by members of the Cheka, the Bolshevik Secret Police. The sinister Jacob Yurovsky led the Cheka in this execution on the nights of the sixteenth/seventeenth of July 1918. To say that the life of a princess is one of privilege does not just refer to the advantages of luxurious living but also the pain that comes when your life belongs to the crown. Bridget could not express her heartfelt sorrows for Princess Beatrice; no words could do justice to the excruciating pain such evilness must have caused her to feel. The household fell silent in disbelief. Four months later, at eleven in the morning on the eleventh day of November 1918, the war would officially end.

"The school of life indeed is a difficult one, but when one tries to live by helping others along the steep & thorny path ones [sic] love for Christ grows yet stronger, always suffering & being almost an invalid, one has so much time for thinking & reading one realizes always more & more that this life is but the preparation to yonder real life where all will be made clear to us."[6]

These feelings expressed by Alexandra in her letter to the Bishop of Ripon prior to her death at the hands of Bolshevik Secret Police's firing squad are so pertinent to the feelings that one experiences once imprinted with the love of a faith in God. When you know in your heart you have been given the grace of a healing miracle or a vision to guide you in your earthly world, it is clear that this path will lead you to a destination for eternity. As a survivor, it was this grace I feel God had given me—the ability to reach deep down into my soul and pull up to the surface my inherited traits that cultivated into the strength I drew from to survive. Be it inherited, learned, or a combination of both, one needs to pull from the graces God has given each of us. We are not identical; we are unique in our traits and graces, but it is up to our "free will" to use what we possess within our own soul to be true.

Bridget and Hamilton's family spent the two years following the war trying to restore their lives back to some normality that resembled their prewar years. They enjoyed their time together on the Isle, playing on the beach and

---

6 Tsarina Alexandra to the Rev. William Boyd Carpenter, Bishop of Ripon, 24 January/7 February 1913. Add .MSS 46721/244, The British Library. As quoted from Gelardi, Julian P. *Born to Rule* (St. Martin Press, New York 2005) p. 178.

picnicking when they were not working. During her first summer back on the Isle in 1919, Bridget had been walking up the avenue on her way to her work at the castle as the soft and gentle wind blew wisps of angelic shapes in the low hanging fog. No one was on the road, only the solitude that filled her mind with quiet thoughts. It had been a long time since she could remember such quietness. Even a weekend on the beach had brought back memories of war in the scent of the freighters on the Channel—the smell of the oil, bitter and black upon the waves. A residue left from the conflict was still unsettling in the minds of the people.

The present turns to the past, leaving an imprint on the soul and mind. Memory should be but is not always reliable; for this reason it should not have so much power over us. During my times of recovery I found a tendency to step out of my happiness and live in those painful memories of the past. The inner soul seems almost to be calling out for a meaning in the pain that can imprint a comfortable familiarity on the soul. In this I share with you, because I have found that sharing my experiences with others is my purpose, and to have a purpose is powerful.

Our DNA passed down to us from generations past has determined not only our physical but also our mental tendencies and characteristics. The way we process and react to our environment and situations has a profound effect on our nature. This nature or imprint will adapt and form new learned behaviors for the survival of self, thus shaping our DNA and passing it on to the children of the next generation.

Once you accept your imprint and the infinite capability

it can possess, you have come face to face with your true nature. Then and only then can your ability to achieve your full potential be given the proper emotional and physical environment. At that point, you can find an inner peace through a better understanding and how best how to deal with the situations you face in your life. Difficult situations have no boundaries—whether they are physical, spiritual, economic, or psychological—and they transcend every level of society—rich or poor, royal or common. Such was the case for my grandparents as they faced poor economic times and the royals, who coped with their own situations in life.

The way we process and react to our environment and situations has a profound effect on our nature. This nature or imprint will adapt and form new learned behaviors for the survival of self, thus shaping our DNA and passing it on to the children of the next generation.

Bridget's warm thoughts of Ireland tucked her in that night as she turned to watch Hamilton sleep, his chest rising and falling with each breath he took. As Bridget lay listening to the crashing waves, she fought sleep to savor the moment, but soon her battle was lost and she gave way, drifting off. The next day the fog had risen with the sun. As she cuddled warmly under the covers, her dream from the night before still lingered in fading memories. Then, tip-toeing to the front door to enjoy the peacefulness of the early morn, she stepped outside. As she took in the scent of the roses mixed with the salty morning breeze flowing gently over the garden, a peaceful nature consumed her.

It was still early when Bridget heard Hamilton stirring, getting ready for his day at the shipyard. She had prepared a nammit (lunch) for him to take to work. Then she put a pot of tea on to boil and began to scramble some eggs. As she stood at the stove he came up from behind, engulfing her in his arms; his smell was sweet and his face freshly shaven. They sat while he savored breakfast, silently enjoying a daily routine that both had missed over the winter. Sometimes the simplest moments are the most cherished. He brushed her cheeks with the tips of his fingers as they found their way under her chin to raise her face to his and kissed her lips. Her eyes followed him as he walked out the door, which closed with a sigh behind him.

The girls were still sleeping as she poured herself another cup of tea. Sitting at the small kitchen table, Bridget caught sight of a mass of grey clouds looming over the horizon. How fast things can change, she thought, recalling the morning sun that had greeted her in the garden but moments ago. How quickly their lives had also changed, for they now expected their third child. Why had all those dreams they had shared that day Hamilton proposed on the beach changed so drastically? They had spent that day in the tearoom, planning their future and gazing into each other's eyes as they had unlocked their souls to each other. The war had separated them and now planning for some stable financial future could mean an even greater and possibly longer separation.

Bridget's mind once again returned to Ireland and

the plight her ancestors had endured during the famine. Families had been ripped apart forever as parents watched their sons and daughters flee their homelands. She told herself, "Be thankful for what you have, Bridget, if this was meant to be, it will only be temporary. The family has struggled through the air raids, rations, and disease of the war and here you are today together." The gale wind blew and the rain came down in slanting sheets as a teardrop fell into her tea cup, creating concentric circles that flowed outward to the cup's edge. She looked up to notice some petals had fallen from a bouquet Hamilton had brought home. A sprinkling of golden pollen left a dusting on the oilcloth covering the table. Sometimes what 'survives' in life is stronger than what has fallen apart.

May 24th, the anniversary of Queen Victoria's birthday, came with the birth of a baby boy named Charles Victor. He had the black curly hair of his Scotch father and the deepest blue eyes of his Irish mother. Born in England, on the Queen's beloved Isle of Wight, at the Princess' request the baby bore her mother's name in its male form with honor.

Soon Bridget would return to work in a slightly diminished capacity for the remainder of the summer, which added to

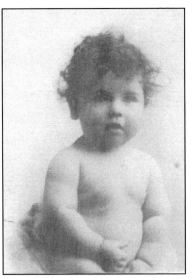

Charles Victor Steen

70

Bridget and her children in London prior to immigrating

Hamilton's need for more work. The summer progressed with the additional stress of yet another mouth to feed and talk of traveling to America became more of a reality for the family. Autumn came on like a whisper from the north blowing in on a cool breeze by the time Bridget returned to London with the royal household. As the holidays approached, it became apparent to Bridget and Hamilton that gifts would be sparse as the monies were tight. There were no new contracts in the shipyards. The shipbuilding trade had always been a feast or famine employment, but since the war, scarcity was overtaking many professions. Odd jobs were far apart and unreliable. They hoped the coming spring would produce some additional work.

The family struggled over the winter and Bridget busied her long nights writing letters to Hamilton when the children slept. She had volumes to share about the children and their lives in London. His ferry rides over from the Isle to the mainland had all but ceased due to the cost.

By spring when the household traveled back to the Isle, an ominous fear had emerged in the pit of Bridget's stomach as she viewed the chalk cliffs, jagged and falling into the sea. It was apparent that Hamilton would have to venture to America in search of a better job. Their earlier way of life would have to change if they were to have any hope for the future.

8

Center of My Labyrinth

ike my grandmother Bridget, my loneliest nights drew me also to prayer, as I lay awake at night wondering if I would ever see my precious little girls grow up to be women. Searching for strength within my inner-self or imprint is a battle I am still enduring—or is it my whole damn war? When you are aware of the way you view yourself and how that view limits you, you will be able to realize the creative source of your behavior. This awareness will allow you to create a new self. When you can honestly assess yourself, you can develop an ability to correct what needs improving. This state of harmony within your self-concept validates reality and leads to a peaceful state of mind. The person you want to be will emerge in you, reflecting back in the mirror of life. At this point you can face life's challenges and your faith will allow you to enter into the unknown with an acceptance that whatever happens, it will be your journey and yours alone. Others may experience their own journey through you, and that is your gift to them, but that journey will be theirs. This grace God gave to all—of understanding and using our imprint. As St. Thomas Aquinas so simply puts it, "Grace builds on nature," as our temperament is part of that nature, and to develop one's self-knowledge is the true importance needed to grow spiritually.

"Self-knowledge is so important that, even if you were raised right up to the heavens, I should like you never to relax your cultivation."
—St. Teresa of Avila

Trying to be proactive in this second battle with cancer instead of reactive, as I had been in my first encounter, I decided to have my long hair cut. This allowed me to grow accustomed to short again before going bald! Joe took me to a hair salon I had never frequented, since we were relatively new in town. I told the stylist my entire situation. When I get nervous or really upset, I tend to talk endlessly, trying to work my anxiety out of my system. In this case, that trait was incredibly helpful, because in the next chair was a woman who very quietly listened to me spew out my troubles. She didn't say a word, but after I left she asked the beautician for my name and number. The next day she called me. Her name was Pam and she was heaven sent—literally. When her son was only two, Pam had been told that she had three short months to live. That had been thirteen years prior.

She had come out of what seemed like an impossible situation. Knowing her treatments would prevent bearing more children, she began helping a young unwed mother who had been kicked out of her home. Later she became a foster mom herself; she turned her death sentence into a life of helping others. Today Pam is a nurse caring for young children and has beautifully raised her own children while helping countless others.

"Friendship is unnecessary, like philosophy, like art, like the universe itself (for God did not need to create). It has no survival value; rather it is one of those things which give to survival."

—C.S. Lewis

Pam's presence gave me someone to reach out to, someone who had experienced the same feelings I had felt before and was now again experiencing. The fear of the unknown was like a labyrinth in my soul as I faced cancer. I imagine that Bridget's turmoil facing her family's separation was similar. As we journeyed down a path in this labyrinth of life to the center of our being, we tried to move forward. Our goal was to create a wonderful life story, triumphing over challenges and gaining the wisdom to walk hand in hand with our spirit to the center of existence and back out wiser than when we started. A labyrinth is a spiritual journey of three stages—the inward journey, the center, and the outward journey. During the inward journey, the self banishes things that hinder our wholeness and inner approach to God. The center is a space of meditative prayer and peace. The outward journey is a relationship with others and with the planet—seen in the light of our relationship with God.

I found myself reaching for the ancestors of my distant family at this point of my journey, alive in their imprints deep in my DNA and soul. They hadn't the technology or capability as I in the twenty-first century, yet must have faced the same illnesses and diseases. I searched for some inner meaning as to the source driving this need to connect with them, so long past in faraway times and distant lands. I didn't have a

The opportunity of the experience is what you gain. It is not a curse. It is a fate that can bring you endless possibilities.

real faith in psychotherapy, but could relate to my religion and that inner spirit fighting to emerge and do battle with the untouched emotions that I had so often ignored. In the past I had always fantasized while absorbed in my innate creativity as an artist and painter. Now as I look back on my battles through the creation of this book, they take on a different form. I have put my paintbrush and canvas aside for a computer. I've replaced pictures for words to express my inner journey as I search my ancestral lineage for an answer to my survival. Where will this all take me? I do not know, but hopefully I will uncover it buried somewhere.

With the same tenacity my grandmother displayed in keeping her family close and the children feeling secure in the absence of their father, I took over my role of commander-in-chief of my body and soul and mother to my household. Once again armed with research on homeopathic cures along with spiritual guidance in my faith, I waged a war with the best possible weapons available to fight this battle. Knowing my daughters could one day be facing breast cancer, I revaluated changes in their eating. When you can personally become an active participant in curing yourself and managing your family's food consumption, you direct your energies in a positive manner emotionally and psychologically. This brings to the foreground a direct link to diet, exercise, and sleep patterns and your body's health, both physically and mentally. It really does help! Fortunately, I was computer illiterate at the time of my cancers, so I didn't go to a website to search out what my survival rate was, nor did I ask any doctor.

In using this book as my form of expression to expose myself as a fellow victim, I am trying to make sense to myself and enlighten readers of what I went through in my battles to achieve recovery and the ongoing battle I face today in my remission period. We all have our own ways to deal with illness. Yet if you are reading this as a caregiver or to gain knowledge through a survivor's eyes, you may want to ponder that you will probably one day be faced with a serious illness. Different illnesses pose different challenges, but the common ground to critical illness is the effects it can have on a life in which loss and suffering will be present. The opportunity of the experience is what you gain. It is not a curse. It is a fate that can bring you endless possibilities.

In my battle with cancer, I found I was not alone as I befriended other victims battling the disease; I formed a camaraderie within a group of survivors. We shared our experiences, hopes, fears, and knowledge of new treatments; we became a form of cancer club. Yet even though we shared a battle, my feelings were mine and mine alone in this unique journey, as were the emotions of my friends and an endless number of other victims. Knowing that a feeling is normal may help some, but that knowledge didn't eliminate what I felt.

My family's summers during this second cancer followed our tradition of time spent at the infamous family cabin in Northern Michigan. A typical "On Golden Pond" purchased by my parents in 1967, it afforded my family a break from our lives in a suburb of Detroit. We had begun spending summers there when I entered my teenage years. My scoliosis forced me to wear a hideous Milwaukee Brace that proved to be equal to a Victorian artifact. Covering from my pelvis to the base of my skull in the back and under my chin in the front, the brace made it impossible to do even the simplest tasks of tying my tennis shoes. This monstrosity of metal bars and leather corset was adjusted through the use of screws and straps—a virtual torture chamber for the body and mind of an active teenager. I was x-rayed every three months and wrenched into a position in an effort to straighten the spine while lowering my self-esteem. My normal teenage interests in clothes, sports, and boys were thrown to the wayside for the twenty-three hours a day I was imprisoned. The twenty-fourth hour was reserved for personal hygiene, hair washing and bathing. To add to these restrictions, the summer became unbearable for one who had spent most waking summer hours at the neighborhood pool. The temperatures in the city climbed, causing skin sores due to the irritation of leather rubbing against sweaty skin. Our northern cottage proved to be a perfect place to retreat. There I worked on my art, played my flute, fished, and enjoyed bonfires at the lake's edge as the brisk breeze coming across the water cooled the night air. History repeated itself with my children, who enjoyed the retreat as a haven while dealing with the ugliness of battling their mother's cancer.

One day at the cottage while I was waiting for my blood counts to rise and taking a break before my upcoming surgery, Joe, the girls, and I boarded our pontoon boat for a day of fishing and swimming. We had stopped at our favorite island to swim off the sandbar and eat our picnic lunch while enjoying the sky's clear brightness and the seagulls' display of aviation skills as they canvassed the water's glistening surface for fish. We decided to venture on a site-seeing cruise around the shoreline, and Frannie, my youngest, amused herself with dropping tidbits of her sandwich bread overboard into the water, coaxing the seagulls to put on a show for her. We were all enjoying the day and the seagulls' ability to entertain us when one bird decided to relieve itself on the brim of my sun hat. We all laughed until I realized that if I removed my hat, my baldness would be displayed in public, a sight I reserved only for the privacy of the shower. It was one of those moments when you laughed until you cried, but for different reasons. I realized my tears were for the reality of the moment in my life and its unpredictable future.

Avoidance could give me a place to retreat when the battle against my disease became too much. I would put my creative juices into full swing and design methods of

attaching fake ponytails and hairpieces to stretchy head-
bands that could be worn under baseball caps and hats. At
one point I actually considered selling my creations. Wigs
are miserable once the temperature climbs over seventy
degrees. Taking what life dishes out and turning it into a
positive way to help yourself and others had a very healing
quality for me.

Sharing my faith gained the most enjoyment for me.
Making rosaries and distributing them when I was at the
hospital for my treatments and surgeries led me down a
path in the early morning hours before dawn after a surgery.
I couldn't sleep so I was pacing the hallway. Upon passing
one room, I noted that a young woman was praying next to
a patient, a young man of about the same age who lay in his
hospital bed asleep and hooked up to all sorts of monitors.
It was apparent that his condition was very serious. I returned to my room and decided to put my sleeplessness to
good use praying for him. I didn't know what faith he had
or if he even had a faith, but I was moved to place one of my
prayer cards and rosaries on his nightstand when his visitor
had left and the nurses were busy making their reports for
the shift change. The next day he received a successful heart
transplant and was graced with the ability to continue his
life with his new bride.

It was little efforts I did, not only for others, but also for
myself to find meaning in this battle I was waging. They
offered peaceful paths to follow. I believed if I helped even
one soul, then this disease I was suffering from had a purpose. For it is in eternity we will be rewarded.

One day not too long after a hospital stay, I received a
call from a woman battling ovarian cancer. Her name was

Gail, and she had met another cancer patient at the same hospital where I had received my surgeries. Gail had witnessed this patient's devotion to the rosary and upon learning of her miraculous cure after a death sentence,

> *Whether you are the victim or caregiver within the family, do not feel you are doing children a favor by keeping important information from them.*

was put in contact with me for instruction. We became friends and through her I also was graced with a strength she shared with me through our friendship. She and her husband together joined the Catholic Church and stood as shining examples to all they came in contact with.

As my grandmother's teardrop caused a series of concentric circles in her teacup that morning on the Isle of Wight, so had one woman's display of her daily rosary moved another to seek out a path not followed in her life as one circle flowed into another. I was with Gail as she prepared to enter into the ripple of her eternal path. She had found meaning and peace to her present state. Isn't that what we all strive for in life? Good-bye, my dear friend.

During my second bout with cancer, my daughter Abagael (the Gaelic form of the name, my attempt at inserting Bridget's heritage) developed separation anxiety possibly due to a very demanding third-grade teacher at a time in her life when she needed loving support. The frequency of my surgeries—five operations in all—and the most horrid chemotherapy brought about painful migraines causing endless hours in bed unable to stand. Many a school day started with a family friend chasing Abagael around our house, and I mean that literally. It was quite a feat with the doublewide lot our house was built on. Once she was caught and buckled into the van, her older sister Sarah held her down and the child guard was engaged on the car doors. It broke my heart seeing the pain in her eyes as she was driven off, but she needed to get away from the cloud that was hanging over our home, and the school day afforded socialization along with educational distractions. The emotional stress for the children of victims is an aspect of the disease that cannot be overlooked.

Whether you are the victim or caregiver within the family of young, teenage, or grown children, do not feel you are doing them a favor by keeping important information from them. It is difficult to handle the balancing act of how to relay information, especially to younger children, and how much to divulge. You have to let your heart be your guide, along with your relationship with the children. Most hospitals offer counseling for this, but don't forget that your involvement is essential. Joe and I found this out at our first experience with a support group. The advice other caregivers gave Joe actually made him take on an overzealous role, hiring help that we really didn't need. This is where you have to self-evaluate your individual needs before you act on them. The advice was good, but we should have only sought sources for necessary help rather than acting on broad recommendations.

9

"Wee Frisson of Fear"

The gale wind blew and the air smelled of salty seaweed as Bridget and her children shuffled off the ferry and unto the dock after crossing the Solent from Southampton. The stanchions of the pier stood strong against the waves, reminding her of her need to display the strength needed for a balance of harmony within her family. The appearance of the lieutenant, a family friend, in place of Hamilton brought a sadness she could not show. He had come to help them back to their duplex. Hamilton was busy working a side job on a fishing boat, checking on the lobster pots in the nearby bays. The duplex greeted her with a warmness she had longed for over the bitter winter. Her garden needed a bit of spring-cleaning, but the appearance of young burgundy buds on the woody stems of her roses was a welcome sign. They revealed their strength to endure as she had braved the long cold months of the past season. Thanking the lieutenant for his help, Bridget busied herself with the job of preparing a lunch for the children and getting them down for a needed nap; they had been up before dawn to make it to the ferry on time.

With the children napping comfortably in their familiar beds, Bridget changed from her traveling clothes into more suitable attire for gardening. She ventured out to the garden to assess what needed her attention. Inhaling the fresh sea air and enjoying the warmth of the sun on her back as she bent over pruning the dead sticks from the rose bushes, Bridget knew she would miss these moments the most should she have to leave the Isle forever. Would they ever be able to find anything that would compare to her home? But she told herself that as long as she and Hamilton and the children were together, her future would work out. In her heart and prayers God would be beside her and she would never be alone if she kept Him close.

That evening when Bridget was in the kitchen preparing a shepherd's pie, Hamilton's favorite dish, she spotted a figure coming up the back road, his silhouette familiar against the golden burnt orange hue of the impending sunset. It was Hamilton with his rubber waders slung over his shoulder and his traditional bouquet of fresh spring flowers. Her heart skipped a beat as she dropped her tea towel and rushed out the back door, down the winding country road, and into his arms. Their souls met at the touch of his rough, strong hands around her waist. Darkness fell behind them as the sun submerged into the western horizon and they strolled back home together in each other's arms.

Hamilton had a job on a fishing boat the next day so Bridget made arrangements with a local neighbor to watch over the children in the early morn so she could go to the market and get needed supplies. Her kitchen had been depleted with the shortage of extra money. She had luckily saved up some extra funds from doing household mending over the winter. It was enough to purchase groceries to stock the shelves. The smoky mist dissolved into ethereal shapes as she walked down the road to town, reminding her of teasing fairies in the Irish tales she had heard long before. At the market on the avenue by the sea, the waves in tides of blue and green shimmered in the dawn's rising sun and created a vision that truly represented the picturesque quality of the Isle. A cluster of gulls swooped down on a school of fish near the glistening surface. An outline of a huge freighter on the horizon caught Bridget's notice on its way out of the pier at Southampton causing a shiver to radiate down her spine. All knew that many an immigrant had ported out of Southampton in search of a new beginning in America. It is the same port from which the *Titanic* sailed on its maiden voyage.

Bridget tried to express the feelings that were overtaking her thoughts that morning as she foraged pantry supplies and hunted for answers to the dark agony that permeated her soul. The ocean felt like a void too vast to cross without being swallowed up. Her agony reared its head like the dragon roaming in the deep waters of Lough Braken Lake. Could she face this fear and slay the beast, overcoming this stay-by-the-hearth grace that was chaining her to the Isle?

Venturing down to the shore, Bridget sought a peaceful

moment by the sea to collect her thoughts. The fishing boats bobbed in the waves as the fishermen's unshaven faces grew dampened with the ocean's spray. The music of the sea radiated from the buoy bells along with the lapping of waves against the ships' hulls. She watched the boats and was soothed by the sound of the breeze rustling the dry beach grass as the scent of the impending rain blew in from the west, encouraging her to begin her return along the esplanade[7].

Summer progressed with an often unspoken sadness about Hamilton's inevitable immigration to the United States. The economic conditions within the shipyards were unchanging, so he prepared to depart in the spring. The unknown is always accompanied by "wee frisson of fear." This was the case with Hamilton's adventure to a foreign country, but it is even more true in the diagnosis of a life-threatening disease and the intense fear of so many unanswered questions. The past is gone, the future is yet to be, and the moment is here and now. The illness, like an albatross, is an encumbrance to be dragged along.

When the season changed, the family continued on apart over the winter. The hardest of all days came as the spring sun rose over the docks in Southampton. There they stood with their little family, Hamilton kissing and hugging his wife and three children with tears in their eyes and hopes in their hearts. Joan was nine, Mollie seven, and Charlie just two. Bridget held the loose end of a red ball of yarn and handed the rest to Hamilton as he boarded the boat. It was customary of the times for the loved one

---

7 esplanade – A walkway by the water's edge.

left behind to hold the end of yarn as the ship vanished in the distance; the unraveling balls left streamers of various colors floating in the wind, signifying the travelers' ties to the homeland. Standing there, Bridget's shoulders began to shake, and the children knew she was crying. A familiar hand rested on her left shoulder and Bridget turned, falling into the arms of her close friend, Maggie. Her heart was breaking, yet she knew their love would survive.

Immersing herself in gaining stability for her family, she took over a lead role in the management of her home.

That spring, it was time to migrate over to the Isle, only Hamilton would not be there to greet them at the docks. Each day Bridget went to the post office in search of a letter from Hamilton. Weeks had passed and still there had been no communication, but letters had to travel on ocean liners back across the Atlantic. Bridget tried to console herself with that fact, though all the while she secretly held a knot in her stomach. One late spring morning before dawn she woke from a particularly pleasant dream. She and Hamilton had been enjoying a sunny day on The Green with the music of a band filling the warm summer air. What had startled her out of sleep? Had it been a mourning dove cooing for a mate? Her waking hours were filled with real-life concerns for her family, but her dream had taken her away from that.

Now on the horizon, the sun rose in a blaze of color as she stepped out into the morning's dawn and a clear blue sky washed away the night's worries. Her small rose garden welcomed her with its blooms opening and reaching toward the rising sun. The roses appeared to smile at her as she entered. Grinning back, Bridget leaned over to catch a whiff of her red 'La Reine' next to the garden gate. The scent of her roses came as whispers forming an image in her mind of the Blessed Mother with a halo of bronze. This vision drew her back to Camp Curragh when she discovered the love that was radiating in her heart and the spirit to 'survive' life's battles. Later that day, a letter arrived with hopes of a new start in a new land. As summer lingered on, more letters arrived with evidence of gainful employment on the railroad in Pennsylvania. Bridget was hopeful they would soon be reunited as a family.

The anguish of life was felt inside Bridget's soul as her mind raced with a mixture of thoughts; some brought coherence while others scattered in a storm of emotion as she prepared to sail for America. Her time on the ocean liner, *Mauritania*—four days, seventeen hours and twenty minutes to be exact—were spent in steerage with the children. They stayed in an area made up of six-to-eight-foot ceilings filled with bunk beds and few bathrooms in the lower level below second class. Charles Dickens commented on conditions in steerage where some seven hundred and sixty-seven immigrants lodged as, "Nothing smaller for sleeping was ever made except coffins." Such accommodations exacerbated the apprehension of her arrival into a new country. In America, an increase in nativism fueled anti-immigration, particularly of Catholics and Jews, which would make even the strongest of women wary under the stress. The downturn in economic conditions was also being felt in America, coupled with the importation of cheap labor and the decline in the national myth of the white Anglo-Saxon self-made man of the 1920s. The concept of "American Dream" was put in print in 1931 when historian James Truslow Adam wrote *The Epic of America*. Bridget's years of service to royalty and the European ideals of class orientation were a strong contrast to Adam's "American Dream" and his words, "…that if we are to have a rich and full life in which all share and play their part, if the American dream is to be reality, our communal spiritual and intellectual life must be distinctly higher than elsewhere, where classes and groups have their separate interests, habits, markets, arts and lives."[8] In her previous life, assimilation did not have a place within society, which made Bridget's view of her identity in this new country one of adjustment.

After shuffling through many hours of questions and inspections on Ellis Island, Bridget could breathe a sigh of relief as she and the children were released. They left on a ferry bound for the train station from which they would travel northwest to the central Pennsylvania town of Renovo, in the Susquehanna River Valley of the Allegheny Mountains.

---

8 Adam, James Truslow, *The Epic of America* (Little, Boston 1931) p. 411

10

Battle Two

uring my second battle and treatment with a new type of cancer, the disease hadn't advanced as far. With the odds of one in a thousand in my favor against lymph node involvement, I was hopeful. However, the odds turned against me when the biopsy of the nodes came back. Since my chest had been radiated to such a high degree from the previous lung cancer, radiation therapy was not an option. After much soul searching and prayer, Joe, my oncologist, and I chose surgery followed by chemo. Due to my previous experience, I elected to have a port put in place to make the chemo treatment easier and less painful.

The surroundings at the hospital were cheery, and I was comfortable with the nurses who had been through this before with me. I always tried to arrive early to get a bed since the drugs made me so drowsy and the other option was an oversized recliner chair. What I wasn't prepared for was the chemo of choice—Adriamycin, a red Kool-Aid-looking drug that produced the most horrid migraine headaches and nausea. At the time, we didn't know that I more than likely had brain tumors silently hiding in my skull causing the migraines. There has been evidence of a connection to breast cancer and meningioma tumors. Second in line to the dreaded chemo treatments and migraines were the regular blood tests. The deadly chemo ate away the good as well as bad cells, which made my veins shrink; inserting a needle became a very painful endeavor.

Because my blood counts had gotten so low and my doctor feared any type of infection I might encounter from a cut, he advised me not to garden. Friends would drop by and help with my Rosary Garden, which I deeply loved. The garden was very fruitful and my perennials flourished and multiplied. Its productivity allowed me to give gardener friends lush, healthy plants during the spring that year, a good way to say thank you. I also hosted an annual table at our church's Advent by Candlelight Tea. I always took great joy in theming my table to go with the food and a thank you gift for each friend who had helped me along the way. One year it was a snowman theme with snowball cookies and a snowman cake. Another year we had Angel Wing Pastries and china angels as gifts. The simple joys in life became major events as I was able to enjoy my garden and host a tea.

Never being a person to procrastinate any endeavor, I approached each new cancer and treatment full force with a positive attitude. The best moments during my battles were when I felt the strong presence with the Lord and when I experienced the kindness of friends who were willing to give of themselves. While in remission for the

second time, I realized that remission is a state of limbo. There
is a level of continual periodic
checkups that comes with a
fear that fluctuates as test results come and go. A survivor's
life is planned out based on the
checkup schedule. Our vacation
plans of booking plane reserva-
tions or hotel accommodations
waited until the test results came
back. My girls are familiar with
this, and many a trip has been

*The generalities
many people want
to place on cancer
victims may
make them fail
to recognize the
differences that
are so important to
what we each need.*

planned around such test results. In my testimonials I give
witness to the fact that we survivors who are afforded life
instead of death now find survival a way of life. Everyday life and endeavors witness the struggles I face today
and tomorrow. Living through this battle and observing
the effects it has on one's life has allowed me to theorize
and form conclusions about what I felt. The purpose of
my writings is to help readers and/or victims bring their
feelings and experiences into a visible light so they can
choose and cope with their own paths to follow. These
paths, available for their journey, are fueled by their free
will and faith.

As a survivor during those post-treatment times, I
would periodically let my mind travel back in time and
would question what might have been had my family not
lived where we were when I was diagnosed with my cancer. Would I have received the proper treatment? Would I
have found the strength in my faith that I needed? Would

I have taken a different treatment path? Would my place here on earth have been able to touch those souls that needed touching with my survival? What would have been? I will never know. All I can hope for at this time is that God's plan was for my life has been of His pleasing and I am forging forward on the path He seeks for me. I know I have fallen many times along the way, but hopefully I will be able to continue down the road to many more crossroads and choose the proper turns. I pray that God has programmed my inner GPS and that my free will follows the correct route.

We cancer victims must fight the disease. Pick up any local newspaper and turn to the obituaries; I bet you will find at least one that reads, "He died after a long battle" or some other reference to the enemy cancer. The term "cancer" is used to depict society's evils such as crime, drug abuse, or any deterioration transforming good into evil. The war against cancer can easily transform the patient into a soldier and his or her life into a battlefield.

God has given each of us a free will; use this time as a wake-up call to reassess your life and strengthen your soul, for it is eternal.

During my battles I felt the loss of my youth being ripped from me at times. You can kid yourself on good days—trying to forget—but the scars from the surgeries and the physical ailments left behind by the chemo and radiation play havoc with you both physically and mentally. I am not sure when it happened, but at one point I realized that my body as I had known it was no more. More likely, I had tried to ignore my physical changes, trying to avoid being as materialistic as the world around me. Our world is bent on trying to seduce individuals into the importance of a fit and youthful figure; it goes far beyond the health aspect to the sexual appeal our body should possess. At this point in my battle, the importance of my soul far outweighed the physical. I didn't know what the future held for my physical body, but I knew that my soul is eternal. With each cancer came new crosses to bear. Many a well-meaning person would comment, "How do you keep fighting?" To this my mind would question the purpose behind such an inquiry. What would they have me do, lie down and die? I think not. If our lives and the values we hold dear aren't worth fighting for, then what is?

Other victims may personify their tumors, even going as far as giving them names. That thought hadn't crossed my mind, but each of us manages our situations differently. No two human beings are alike—we are all individuals—and should not be placed in the group or stage based on a hypothesis. The patient may find reassurance in knowing that others have felt the same way or have experienced similar circumstances, but it is wrong to get caught up in just accepting the norm. The generalities many people want to place on cancer victims may make them fail to recognize the differences that are so important to what we each need. My friend Pam and I are two soldiers who waged our own battle against the norm and came out victors. She knew her odds; I chose not to because I was determined to be different. In this, my age-old stubbornness or tenacity showed itself.

I found the greatest strength I held was in visualizing

my cancer as the devil. He was present, trying to end my life or keep me from waging my battle against the sins he inflicted on my soul and that of others. I tried to bring out the "strength within." Emotionally and physiologically, I pulled on my inner being or imprint to immerse my soul in God. I asked Him to give me the strength and knowledge to bring others to Him so they might find peace and trust in whatever the future holds. This gave my disease a purpose. The future is beyond our control. I once knew a man who watched all his pennies; he planned his life so carefully for the future that he missed out on the present. But in retirement, when he was ready to enjoy the fruits of his labor, he was killed in a bus accident while on one of his planned adventures. God has given each of us a free will; use this time as a wake-up call to reassess your life and strengthen your soul, for it is eternal. You will reap many rewards, for this I am certain—no matter what the future holds on this battlefield.

11

War

It is only fitting that at this time I travel to December 7, 1941, to the shores of Pearl Harbor and an attack that hurled our nation into a war of necessity. It is a day that we as human beings throughout our world must not let ourselves forget. "And sometimes remembering will lead to a story, which makes it forever. That's what stories are for joining the past to the future. Stories are for those late hours in the night when you can't remember how you got from where you were to where you are. Stories are for eternity, when memory is erased, when there is nothing to remember except the story."[9] Memory can weaken with age and time. In this time of unrest and turmoil in the Middle East, we must not be propelled again into what may become the final or most deadly holocaust this earthly world may witness.

---

9 O'Brien, Tim. *The Things They Carried* (Houghton Mufflin Harcourt Publishing Company, New York 1990)

*From now on it is only though a conscious
choice and through a deliberate policy that
humanity can survive.*

—Pope John Paul II

Working as a machinist apprentice in the railroad shops
of P.R.R. in Renovo, Pennsylvania, Charlie, as my father
liked to be called, was awaiting his call to duty. He had one
year of college under his belt and the economic need to further his education had created the necessity of work. The
inevitable call to duty in service of the country waited just
around the corner on Huron Ave. as the local barber shop
even sported a sign announcing, "NO YELLOW BELLIES
NEED ENTER." The souls of American men swelled with
anger and a fearless desire to enlist in a war that had dared
to touch our soil. When the pull to become a patriot was
too strong to bear, Dad traveled to Harrisburg with two of
his close friends, Bud Saib and Buddy Pearson, to enlist. He
was then informed of a hernia he was previously unaware
of. This condition swung the pendulum into an unpredictable turn of events. Classified 4F, or medically unfit for duty,
when patriotism was running very high all over the country,
labeled him "draft dodger." This stigma stuck to him as long
as he stayed within the small mining town.

Bridget and Hamilton felt that their children's enlist-
ment in the Armed Forces and Nursing Corps sealed their
citizenship in their new country in the eyes of their neigh-
bors, who hadn't been overly friendly upon their arrival as
immigrants. Surviving many hard times and living through

World War I in England—a war that hadn't touched American soil—had forged a trust in their faith and destiny.

Young Charlie had no patience for the overwhelming single-mindedness that possessed the American girls being left behind. Jenny, a black Irish Catholic beauty with dauntingly blue eyes and light freckled skin who had set her sights on him proclaimed, "If you go you may get killed and with death you will miss out on life and all it has to offer you here."

Charlie responded, "Well then, I better go if the American way of life is so important!"

"What about our religion, Thou shall not kill?"

He knew the answer, but in 1942 there was no place for it. To quote my father's memoirs, "It is strange how people think, but when members of a family are killed or wounded they have no compassion. Little square flags with a blue star in the center hung in the windows showing that a member of that family was in the service. When the flag changed and a gold star appeared it meant that a service person had been killed." He desperately wanted to enlist, so through the help of his sister, Mollie, a Second Lieutenant in the Nurse Corps, he made arrangements with a doctor in Philadelphia. Mollie knew he would keep the price of hernia surgery low for Charlie. The cost became one my father could bear with the sale of his prized 1937 DeSoto for $250, thus making it possible to enlist in August of 1942.

Of the twelve billion soldiers who went to war, Charlie knew he was just a body, and whoever he had been in Renovo was of no difference in the world. The Germans, with unmerciful cruelty, were winning; the Japanese still ruled the Pacific as his new life in the Army began in a branch called Coast Artillery. Within a week, he was on a train bound for San Francisco with about five hundred men. A two-month training period commenced before he was sent to Alaska where he set up coastal guns in case the Japanese, who were in the Aleutian Islands, tried to enter the Alaskan Territory. Once the guns were in place, Charlie went to work stringing telephone wire to the gunners for communication and operating the field switchboards. These switchboards and field phones were carried in slings and canvas cases powered by flashlight batteries. Everything was portable to move quickly. Before being sent to Europe he was placed at Sitka Air Base. The Army's job at the base focused on firing permanent guns at any Japanese invasion fleet. Charlie was in charge of checking lines to the guns, operating the switchboard, and manning searchlights in case of an air attack. Dad remembered how the time seemed to drag on in Sitka with its misty cold and rainy climate that went on for days on end. Comments like getting the "Alaskan Stare" and the possibility of the guys talking to themselves appeared within the pages of his memoir written years later. In an effort to be where the action was, a group of approximately thirty men boarded a boat for Juneau to test for positions in Air Cadet Training. Charlie was selected for bombardier training and sent to Canyon State Teachers College. Then one day during a training session, Air Corporal General Arnold informed the men that due to the low numbers of casualties, they were being sent back to Alaska.

A change of plans came early in the morning when the train my father was riding back to Alaska made an unscheduled stop. From the front and rear cars soldiers boarded the train announcing, "You're not in the Air Corps anymore; you're in the infantry. Welcome to Camp Grueber, Oklahoma." The men were well aware of the foot travel and front-line combat this change meant. However, they didn't know that all across the United States, men were being thrown into the infantry for the coming invasions of Europe and Japan.

Charlie in uniform

My father was assigned to a Headquarters Company of the Third Battalion in the 242nd Infantry Regiment of the 42nd Rainbow Division, composed of wiremen, radiomen, and message-center personnel. Training started in "The Badlands" outside Muskogee, Oklahoma. It included fourteen-mile hikes with full field packs, rifle, and ammunition. The trainees crawled under barbed wire while "live ammunition" was fired overhead. In November 1944, the men boarded a boat proceeding down to the east coast destination of Marseilles in southern France. After ten days of dodging German submarines, the infantry landed in France and set up tents ten miles outside town. Before traveling to the front lines, the soldiers were given a twelve-hour pass. Upon returning they found that a German plane, had bombed the area. No one was hurt, but the tents were ruined. "Welcome to the front line of combat!"

The grapevine foretold that the three regiments that had arrived with Charlie's group had no support troops, artillery, quartermaster for supplies, and ordinance for vehicle repair. The only help might possibly come from the 79th Division; otherwise they were on their own. The backup troops, they learned, were still stateside in New Jersey at Camp Kilmer. The men were eventually sent to the Maginot Line, a French fortification that hadn't stopped the Germans two years before. Lines were laid for the arriving rifle companies, mortar company, and headquarters. Food was in short supply—three boxes of K-rations per day, which were small enough to fit inside their jacket pockets. After flame-throwers burned some of the men, they were ordered to dig a "foxhole" in the ground; it would be home for the next month. The sleeping bags hadn't come, so each man received one blanket. Pine boughs covered by their ponchos sufficed as mattresses.

When a line went out, a solider left in the dark of the night to find the trouble. Sometimes the Germans cut lines and lay in wait for an ambush or placed a mine or grenade under the wire. By mid-December, the snow had started to fall. Rumor had it the Germans had broken though just north of the regiment in a place called Bastonge. One night word came to make a quick retreat. Everything but the switchboard was left behind. It was bitterly cold and the snow quickly covered the ground as the wind ripped at the soldiers' total physical beings, but the adrenalin rushed the men forward in a fleeing mass. Seeking out a deserted home for shelter, Charlie and his men set up the switchboard in the basement as the Germans started attacking. The rifle companies took a beating but held their position. A week passed and the front lines straightened out, allowing the men to travel to Legarde, France, after being relieved by the 36th Division from Texas. A much needed shower and shave after a month in their foxhole was a pleasant privilege.

Coming to this time in my father's life, I can't help but wonder what thoughts overtook him down deep inside his earthen hole, hiding as would a hare from a fox. He was a man wanting to fight, but fearing for his life. The hole was probably not just a place to cower as it was a spot to retreat for solace, and to ponder his imprint as he battled this enemy. Did his thoughts drift back to his grandfather fighting the Boer War for his namesake queen? Or to his peasant ancestors starving during the famine that besieged Ireland? Or was he experiencing the same fear I was in my battle with my enemy, cancer? Fear is fear—we all have it—we just deal with it. We journey in this life, some better than others, as we forge our own paths, climb our own hills, and ride out the bumps.

From the rear, troops arrived to replace the men they had lost. A new man, Dusty from Kalamazoo, Michigan, who had never witnessed combat, was assigned to Dad. They would look out for each other as brothers on this team of warriors. In the end of January 1945, the men returned to the front in Wimmenau, Germany, at the base of the Hardt Mountains. The worst battle was yet to come. In the early hours of a dreary morning mist, as the damp chill of the breaking spring cut through the soldiers' ponchos, the Germans attacked their regiment from all sides. They were soon pinned down in a meadow at the base of a mountain. The meadow had previously been mined, and the rifle companies falling into the trap were in bad shape.

They were stuck in the meadow, mortared without cover. A battalion aid station, usually in the rear, found a way to move up with much needed plasma for the injured. Every soldier outside the meadow became a litter bearer to carry the wounded into a temporary aid station to be pumped with blood and hopefully given a jeep ride to the rear. The battle continued for ten long hours.

When the Germans needed additional supplies, they finally began to retreat. An officer and his radioman were sent out to check on their position. When the men were later reported missing, Charlie and three wiremen volunteered to form a search party. They laid down wire to keep an up-to-date communication going as they crawled on their bellies through the dark, mountainous terrain still burning from the phosphorous shelling of the battle. Cautiously they searched, avoiding German patrols still occupying the area. A rough idea of the officer's last radio report led Charlie to the two men. Directing them safely back to camp resulted in my father's second Bronze Star for bravery. The first had come from a previous attack on his jeep, which permanently embedded scrap metal into his leg. He recovered in the rear and returned to duty. These medals, along with others, are proudly displayed under glass on my husband's office wall. Dad never earned a world-renowned solid gold cup like his father. But his medals were far superior in my eyes, those of his family, and hopefully his nation.

The next day, after emerging from the cover of the mountains, the regiment witnessed the destruction done by the Air Corps to the retreating German troops. Using horses to pull their guns as a result of insufficient fuel, the Germans became sitting targets for the American aircraft, which had bombed and strafed the retreat. Dad's memoirs reveal those moments sealed within his memory; he recalled the nausea as vomit ascended in the back of his throat and his stomach heaved at the sight of war. The adrenalin rushing through his veins from the night before had subsided and was replaced with thoughts of what could have been in that now peaceful mountain meadow.

The problem in defense is how far you can go without destroying from within what you are trying to defend from without.
—Dwight D. Eisenhower

Wurtzburg was the soldiers' next objective and it took three days of fighting to capture the city. As the Germans retreated, hotly pursued by our troops, the roads looked like *The Grapes of Wrath*. The American soldiers picked up cars, bikes, and trucks as they marched forward; no one walked. The end of the war was in sight. Many had died, and others would wear scars for the remainder of their lives—if not physically, within their souls. Hopefully there exists an interface and escape route between the physical life and the soul.

The men covered fifty miles in less than a day, slowing only for encounters with stubborn German troops not so willing to give up. Many Germans surrendered, and the Americans built makeshift stockades to contain those captured until the rear troops arrived to guard them before shipping them off to prisoner-of-war camps. Resistance was slight, and the 242nd Infantry kept moving on to

Nuremburg, the site of Hitler's rallies. The 15th Air Force out of Italy was to bomb Schwienfurt, the next city on the list to overtake. As the men stood on a hill outside the city, B-24 Liberators flew over and dropped their bombs. As the final insults fell on the nation once led by a vicious, evil leader who would take his last breath at his own hands in his study at Fuhrerbunker, my father and his fellow soldiers advanced to the site of one of Hitler's worse atrocities, the concentration camp of Dachau.

In my father's memoirs there is a loss of words to describe the terrible inflictions one group of human beings can inflict on others. Witnessing the death of the enemy, civilians, and fellow GIs was overshadowed with the horror of what lay beyond the gates of Dachau. The large, locked, forbidding iron gates displaying the German swastika were opened as the prisoners with their sallow faces, whitened skin, and empty, sunken eyes ran, walked, limped, or were carried out. They were clothed in skullcaps and rags striped in black and dark grey with makeshift shoes or barefoot. As the Americans approached, SS Guards tried frantically to dress themselves in the clothing off the sadly departed prisoners who were unable to last until liberation came. Charlie and two fellow soldiers came upon a prisoner pinning back the arms of a man while another was pulverizing his body with bare fists. Blood spewed from his nose and mouth as a young girl stood to the side witnessing the beating. The girl's eyes revealed a hatred that would burn forever in my father's memory, even though it was an image he wished had left him. With their broken German, the American soldiers learned that the victim was really an SS guard who had killed the girl's boyfriend the day before. Immediately stripping the shirt from his body, the soldiers revealed his tattooed SS symbol. Sealing a death sentence, they left him to the prisoners' assault. Dad's confession tells of a war and what the soldiers witnessed around them, which led to their decision to let the SS guard pay for his actions against these sad people whose wounds were immeasurable.

They count as quite forgot,
They are as men who existed not,
Theirs is a loss past loss of fitful breath,
It is the second death.
—Thomas Hardy

The gates of Dachau revealed such atrocities as huts where victims were locked up by the guards en masse while machine guns shredded the walls; ovens opened to stretchers with rollers for body burning; and boxcars loaded with the dead awaiting the bulldozers to dig mass trenches of graves. After witnessing the horror, a general traveling with the rear troops went to the village and ordered the civilians to come to the camp and carry the bodies out of the boxcars to bury them. That night Dad and his men kicked a German family out of their home. The family tried to vindicate themselves of the crimes that had gone on but a few kilometers away from their farmhouse. In my father's words, "We had seen too much to listen."

The next day, inmates from the camp could be found wandering the countryside, not knowing where to go.

American soldiers heading on to Munich and Saltzburg gave out K-rations with their prayers, doing what they could to help displaced persons trying to survive. As the soldiers were finally receiving hot chow, starving children waited by the garbage cans for their leftovers. Many a man ate ever so little in an effort to help the youngsters. Ropes were strung with blankets to try to give families some separation to exist against the elements. Word came of Hitler's suicide in Berlin. The SS and other supporters attempted to flee to South America or hide arms and money in the Alps.

Charlie was assigned to the small village of Hopfgarten to set up communications. There he was lucky enough to get the job of driving a jeep to a local brewery to keep the camp supplied. This break from the burdens of the war gave his mind distance to recoup, creating a mist covering the memories and softening the sharp, jagged blade that had cut at his soul.

Finally, November 1945 came; before the first snowfall could cover the ground, the chill of what had been left behind found a place in my father's soul. Some would return home intact, but others had been separated physically for all eternity. A letter arrived as my father prepared to set sail from LeHarve, France. His best friends, Bud and Buddy, who had entered the armed forces on that day so long ago in Harrisburg when they had boarded a train to enlist, would not be in Renovo to reunite when he returned. They were counted among the gold stars so many families proudly displayed in the name of Freedom. Walking down Eleventh Street to his family's duplex upon his return, Charlie realized that he had not killed on the battlefields of Europe for some ideal. He had killed to stay alive. After being so eager to enlist to show his patriotism, he had changed after those months in foxholes and on the front. He had seen too much. His inner strength to fight had only returned when he saw the residue of terror in the sunken eyes of Dachau. It was a war of necessity.

"Let every nation know, whether it wishes us well or ill, we shall pay any price, bear any burden, meet any hardship, support any friend, oppose any foe, to assure the survival and success of liberty."

—John Fitzgerald Kennedy

Now came the recovery the soldier experiences as he tries to readjust to life back home. The damage of war wounds were not evident on Charlie's body in the way I see mine in the mirror each morning, but I knew that my father understood my recovery period, for he had experienced his own. Sometimes the invisible marks we hold inside are harder to endure. No one sees or feels them—only the survivor. Those around you don't understand why you aren't going through your day with a persevering smile painted on your face. The blessing is felt inside my soul; it is the learning to journey down another path that is so hard to adjust to.

I accept that my father has forever passed from this world as I know it. The ability to seek answers to questions I may no longer ask of him has passed on. His death left my children and I with an imprint that we will forever hold dear in our hearts. He was a man, father, grandfather, and soldier who passed into God's hands on the anniversary of the fall of the

Twin Towers. On September 11, 2006, Charles Victor Steen became an imprint within our memory. It is a date I am sure he would be proud to have marked his passing as his 42nd Rainbow Division brothers stepped up to aid and assist the country once again in New York City's time of need.

A man born to a humble servant in the presence of royalty, he was bestowed the namesake of one of the world's most famous queens. As a toddler, Charlie would travel to his new country in the bellows of steerage aboard an English ocean liner to then walk hand in hand with his mother through the halls of Ellis Island. Yet his family held within their hearts a loyalty and gratitude to Great Britain's "Last Princess," Beatrice, who made their immigration possible. Though new quotas limited the number of immigrants, Beatrice personally requested visas from the newly assigned Secretary of State, Frank Kellogg.

Charlie would risk his life during 1942-1945 on the battlefields of Europe, witnessing the horrors of war, the destruction of lives, and the cruelty one human being can inflict on another. If we are to value the imprint our lineage has on our lives today as Americans, we cannot neglect the hardships and deeds of our forefathers.

This chapter in my journey has brought me back in time to four years ago. My daughter's wonderfully dedicated teacher realized the need to document the experiences of a WWII soldier. She encouraged my daughter and an upperclassman from her high school to put my father's story on film. Upon his death a few short months after the interview, a twenty-one-gun salute with full military honors would bring an earthly conclusion to his life for all to witness.

12

Battle Three

he unknown and the waiting is the nightmare. There is comfort in knowing all the answers. With the results, there is clarity, which allows you to know what you are fighting. It is a funny thing; cancer, like war, is a battle that has no limits to the causalities it takes. There are no plans to bomb civilians, but the longer the war lives on it forms a mind of its own. Cancer cells create new forms immune to the drugs. They give false remission results to lie in hiding, waiting for their moment in time to raise their angry heads and ambush the unaware survivor.

It was that way with me on my third cancer. Knowing my body better than anyone, I wanted to believe the doctors that everything was cancer free, but my gut told me otherwise. I had by now learned to listen to my body; I wished I had heeded the signs when I first felt something was wrong a year and a half before my first diagnosis. It was at that time when doctors tried to prescribe cough and nasal sprays, and I listened to their theories on allergies and the famous "New House Sick House" handout on all the hazards a newly built home may have. It detailed chemicals in new paint, carpet, plastic laminates, plaster, draperies, etc. and the odors they release into the air. It

> *All too often patients hide from their fears and only share their concerns with the medical profession. They are denying themselves the exchange of personal experience with others who are dealing with the disease.*

seemed to make sense, but while we were distracted by that theory, I progressed to stage three non-small cell lung cancer—not a pretty sight.

This time around, my doubtful physician questioned my concern saying, "If it will make you feel better, we'll order a CT, but we don't feel there is a need." Having been through two previous cancers, I knew the games my mind could play on my fears and appreciated the doctors' insights. Unfortunately, my all-consuming fear of a reoccurrence proved justified as everyone fell silent looking at the CT results. They revealed a small cancerous lesion between the upper and middle lobes of my right lung. This physician now uses my case to teach young interns the need to take the time to listen to patients' concerns. I was quickly scheduled for surgery as my persistence had only let this enemy reach stage one. I needed no follow-up chemo or radiation this time, but gave up two more lobes of my right lung.

It was the Lenten period, and Easter Sunday was in sixteen days. During this time I abstained personally while rekindling my memories of my first lung cancer four years prior, also during Lent. At a time when we Christians remember the Passion of our Lord and the cross He carried for our sins, it's important to remind ourselves of the crosses we must carry to truly experience life in its abundance. To be a witness of only the joys in life is to live in a fairy tale and not the real world. Our precious moments are the results of our ancestors' blood and sweat before our time and the imprints they have created within us.

After I learned of my scheduled surgery the following week, I went to Father John's novena to discuss my commitment to give a testimonial on Divine Mercy Sunday, which was in two weeks. I was torn between my promise to our Lord to spread the word of the miracle I was graced with and my ability to stand in front of the parish and speak after such a short recuperation from lung surgery. I was familiar with the drugs for pain and the resulting weakness from the decreased amount of oxygen my body had to adjust to. Being an optimistic Polish man like my husband Joe, Father John said he had complete faith in my ability to speak and planned to be with Joe and me in the hospital before the surgery. Who could not give this devout and dedicated priest an honest, heartfelt attempt?

Recouping in my hospital bed after surgery, I realized I could barely speak because of my shortness of breath. What was I to do? When Father came to visit the next day, I had to whisper my concern, but once again he reassured me. He comforted me with the fact that I had already typed up my testimony for his approval the week before I knew about the reoccurrence of cancer. If on that Sunday I couldn't complete my talk, a friend could take over. He obviously had a deep faith in my ability—more than I had in myself.

With Father John's faith in me, I focused on my promise to spread Jesus' word during the time I had to prepare. As I took the podium that Sunday, a mere ten days later, Jesus took hold of my voice, and it responded strong and joyous for all to hear of the faith we should have in placing our trust in the Lord. A miracle had once again been granted for the parish to witness. This time the miracle came in the form of a loud and strong voice declaring the works that can happen when you trust in the Lord. My family's faces fell white when they witnessed the return of my voice. Unbeknownst to me, in the audience was a terminally ill patient from out of town who had heard about Sunday's testimonials. The news of his attendance was relayed to me afterwards at my post-op appointment because we shared the same wonderful oncologist. The testimonials had brought him peace, and isn't that what we all strive for in our battles?

When I was initially diagnosed with cancer, my father-in-law and mother-in-law, Berney and Mary, took me to a small chapel built by a woman who had a miraculous recovery from a critical illness. She gave me three holy medals to start my journey: St. Anne, my patron saint; St. Aquinas, saint to educators; and St. Peregrine, saint to cancer victims. I attached my medals to a bracelet that my mother had acquired during her time in the Red Cross helping with the war efforts during World War II. This journey gave way to experiences as numerous as the struggles our daily lives produce, some more eventful than others. Recompense for all that I have gained exists in favors granted, friendships formed, and most of all, the faith restored and gained anew. As a visual path on this journey of mine, my friends added holy medals to my bracelet, which I proudly wear and will always cherish.

After the battle, you will never choose to return to the oblivion where you were before your diagnosis. This lesson came at too great a price, and the young and healthy have never lived through this perspective. Wanting to carry all the knowledge gained through my suffering, I remember asking God to grant a cure, but to never let me forget what I had learned in the experience. I may have been given

Wanting to carry all the knowledge gained through my suffering, I remember asking God to grant a cure, but to never let me forget what I had learned in the experience.

that grace each and every time a new tumor was found. Now I carry with me two meningioma brain tumors and the only problem with looking toward recovery comes in the reality that I may not recover.

As a victim in this battle, one must seize each opportunity to talk or write about it. Speak out to others who are battling cancer or caring for victims. Share your experiences to educate society. In accepting the illness I live differently. It was as hard for me to fight through cancer as it has been to let go and move on. I tend to live in the past with a fear of recurrence, or I try to forget it ever existed, which is against my own advice because it lets my hard-fought victory slip away. In recovery it is important to recognize that the illness didn't just happen to me—the victim. Those around me were also affected and they needed time to deal with it as well.

It meant a great deal to surround myself with people who had experienced the same battles or were undergoing them with me. In those relationships I found all too often friends who could not travel on in this life with me, but they have won my unrelenting love and admiration in the way they handled their last moments with those who shared their experience. Of this I am eternally grateful. Their lives have left an unending imprint within the DNA of their children and in the effects they had on the lives around them. Goodbye, my dear friends. It is my hope that one day I can go out with as much grace as you. Life isn't eternal but our imprints are.

It is important for everyone—victim, survivor, and caregiver—to enlighten themselves and their souls on the unforgettable journey of experiences they are about to or may have already endured. The narrative may not be of the illness itself as it is the experiences of the illness. I gratefully share my memories of the moments and situations I ventured to through my cancer.

Society has fortunately changed its expectations regarding cancer patients. In the past, the diagnosis of cancer meant impending death. This was my interpretation back in 1998 when I was first diagnosed with non-small cell lung cancer. At that point, I had not known anyone who survived the dreaded disease, since my family wasn't familiar with the illness within our gene pool. A phenomenon has occurred with patients like myself not accepting death and battling to take charge and helping themselves through alternative means.

I didn't disregard my doctor's advice; I only tried to be an active participant in the war to survive. I devoured all the books I could on alternative holistic methods. I became a frequent customer at our local health food stores, where a wide array of vitamins and suggestions were plentiful. I found that I had to let go of old habits and attitudes that caused my life to encounter stress. Stress affected my health far more than I realized. When stressed I would tense my muscles, my heart would race, and my relationships would falter.

I need to tell others of my experiences so that I may in some way touch them. All too often patients hide from their fears and only share their feelings and concerns with the medical profession. They are thus denying themselves the exchange of personal experience with others who are dealing with the disease or will at some point in their lives. Putting aside the importance of talking about hopes and fears and how to face the real prospect of death, one loses the chance to touch a fellow human being. I have no sure-fire answers to coping; I can only share how my friends, family, and I dealt with my illnesses as well as the afflictions of our friends.

13

The Generations

y mother's childhood was one of economic security but void of her parents' presence. They both had died suddenly, days apart, one month after the stock market crash of 1929 and the beginning of the Great Depression. They left behind seven children, ages eighteen to nine, to manage under the guidance of lawyers. My grandfather, Harry Batschelet, had run a lucrative business and established trust funds for his family. Kate, my mother, was only eleven at the time.

For Kate, memories of growing up were filled with walks in the mountains where the autumn trees were the brightest golds and the fieriest reds. Her brother Fred was her constant companion, and on the last afternoon they spent together, the weather was warm and the waft of pines hung in the air after a short cloudburst. There was a patchy mountain mist, and the amiable clouds streaked the approaching evening sky with violet and rose as if descending from heaven. He talked of the days when they were younger and would misbehave. The past is sometimes almost as much a work of the memory as the imagination is of the future.

"If father took the strap to me or mother sweetly reprimanded me, I would sulk in my room until you would coax me out," confided Fred.

"I remember getting you to play plunk the can with our 22s in the mountain behind the hotel when Father caught you teasing Trudy with a dead toad."

"I can still see Trudy's face when she opened her lunch tin at recess and saw that old dead toad!" They shared a good long laugh as they dawdled up the mountain path.

Fred and Kate were just a year apart in age and her tomboy ways made her an excellent sidekick for her brother. They were almost inseparable until that terrible day after the dentist pulled his bad tooth and the poison that had abscessed spread through his bloodstream, killing him. There were no antibiotics back then, and some infections were unstoppable. The family suffered again as another member was taken from them, but no one more than Kate.

Life without Fred held emptiness; as she entered high school, she outgrew her tomboy ways and replaced them with more athletic tendencies that were not like those of any of her sisters. Nonetheless, she tried out for the cheer squad and, with her small build and daredevilish ways, she wasn't afraid of being tossed in the air or climbing to the top of the human pyramid. These attributes made her a good choice. She first met Charlie in the gymnasium of Renovo High School. He was the youngest member on the varsity basketball team when Kate was a varsity cheerleader. When they were teenagers, he had asked out her younger sister, Trudy, but Charlie and Kate found a mutual attraction for each other after he returned from the war years later.

When Charlie was young, he spent a great deal of time watching and admiring the basketball skills of the young men on the YMCA basketball court. The location at Third Street and Huron soon became his second home. It provided safe housing, healthy activities, and spiritual support to the men who lived and worked in the town. The organization was supported by the Pennsylvania Railroad and offered its employees educational courses. Both the YMCA and the Elks Club became social organizations that gave Charlie and many of his friends a good sound moral base to draw from, one he continued throughout his adult life.

One day after cheer practice, Kate was strolling past Batschelet's Row, one of her father's real estate adventures that had made their lives quite comfortable. With her senior year ending, her thoughts were drawn to her future choice of plans. As she caught her reflection in Darrin's Poolroom window, she caught the sight of men young and old, generations that had not ventured past the mountains enclosing this small town. Then, gazing though the windowpanes of the Renovo Produce Market, she spotted women, some with youngsters in tow, who were selecting the ripest strawberries, fresh in on yesterday's train from down south. They had exhausted their supply of last year's preserves, and Mrs. Edleine was purchasing her famous meatloaf ingredients. This commonplace small-town life she knew was not to be her destiny, yet what was? Then making the turn on Erie, she walked past more establishments and stopped to scan the Five-and Dime's window, but nothing caught her eye. It was four o'clock and the whistle blew for the next train leaving the depot headed east, possibly to such exciting cities as Philadelphia or even New York.

"Hey Kate!" yelled Jomarie, her friend from the cheer squad; she was with her boyfriend, a varsity basketball player, in his father's Nash. "Come join us—a group of seniors are meeting up at the soda shop on Fifth Street." Kate left her thoughts behind and slid in to take a backseat next to Ginny, another varsity cheerleader.

The shop was hopping and the jukebox cranked out tunes by Tommy Dorsey, Fred Astaire, and Bing Crosby. She spotted her sister Trudy and some of her friends in a back booth enjoying chocolate and cherry cokes. She smiled and waved, noticing a young man she had seen on the basketball court several times. They hadn't been formally introduced but in this small town she knew he had come from England with his family when he was young and had attended St. Joseph's until high school. His thick wavy black hair and robin-egg-blue eyes had always been attractive to her, but he was in Trudy's grade and high-school girls of her status never dated younger boys, though he was quite the ballplayer.

Graduation came and went; it had been a good year with many memories and decisions. The fall would bring the University of Michigan and the beginning of a new dawn with life outside the boundaries of Renovo. Little did she know what was brewing in distant lands, a long way away from the Allegheny Mountains.

Kate as a Red Cross volunteer

Events beyond both the Pacific and Atlantic would pull her across the country as a volunteer in the Red Cross to do her part in the war efforts. With her volunteer work, Kate would travel as far as Texas helping with social and sport activities on base camps. She earned her degree in Physical Education in 1940 and found a meaningful way to use her background.

The day Charlie returned to Renovo with other soldiers from all positions of the Armed Forces was one of great celebration for the small town. There was a parade, and the high-school band played at the station on Erie Avenue. Among the crowd were Bridget and Hamilton to greet their son, Kate, and the entire town of Renovo citizens. Months later, Kate and her sister Trudy moved to Michigan, where Kate found employment and Trudy married the only son of a prominent family from Grand Rapids. The young couple would sadly enjoy only a brief marriage before the groom was shot down over the Pacific in the Korean War, never to be found. During trips home to visit Renovo, Kate and Charlie enjoyed a short courtship. They were both anxious, like so many young couples, to put the lost years of wartime behind them.

The fact that my parents' families were of opposite ends of the socioeconomic ladder always bothered my grandmother Bridget. It probably stemmed from her years of working for royalty, which created the Victorian view of the upper class not mixing with the common folk. It had been her way of life since childhood and one she had grown to accept. She always felt my mother was attracted to my father for the thrill of dating the boy from the other side of the tracks who had come home as a decorated war hero. As she grew older, Bridget became very set in her ways. She had a demeanor no one wanted to challenge. She was a very class-orientated Irish Catholic who knew the hardships of her place in the United Kingdom and had faced similar circumstances once she reached the United States. Within her own family Bridget ruled with the hand of a matriarch, much the same as Princess Beatrice and her mother, the Queen. This situation was not the ideal relationship Kate had hoped for with Charlie's mother, but it was one she respected.

One December night, Kate stepped from the passenger train onto the platform and looked around with an ever-present hint of mischief in her hazel eyes. She was emotionally drained instead of physically tired from her travel home from her alma mater, University of Michigan in Ann Arbor. She was now employed at the neighboring college of Michigan State Normal. As she walked briskly along Erie Avenue, street lamps—an improvement made by the Renovo Borough Council—lighted her way. She felt her mind slowing down as soon as she stepped off the train. Getting through the demanding month of finals in grad school and work were hard enough. The clogging residue of her world came flowing back as she trudged through the snow and slush on the Avenue. She had an innate impulse to run toward Drury's Run to a safe place inside her soul.

Renovo and Ann Arbor were antipodes of each other. The lively intellectual atmosphere in the cafes and restaurants on Main Street in the college town contrasted with the slow-paced, family-centered life in the quaint mining town in the mountains. Many of her friends and family desired to venture to bigger cities and the life they might provide. Such was the case with her sister Billy, who traveled off to marry a prominent East Coast doctor. Kate also had spread her wings, but the return to the small town, especially during the holidays, always brought with it a homey, secure comfort. This Christmas she anticipated Charlie was going to propose marriage. Their long-distance relationship needed to change if it was to flourish. After the war, he had worked in the railroad shops at a job his father had gotten him but he longed to return to college. With Kate's employment as an instructor and Trudy moving out of the apartment they had shared in Michigan, it was the opportune time in their lives to tie the knot and move on to the next level in their relationship. Charlie could attend U of M while she continued her work.

Caught in her thoughts, Kate's attention was drawn to the present by the blaring horn from Harry's new Packard. Harry, her older brother, along with Amy, the eldest of the Batschelet clan, had almost single-handedly raised their younger siblings. They had stepped into their parents' shoes, remaining in town to run the family business. Harry had gotten married, and his siblings decided he should be given the West Branch Hotel in which to raise his family. Amy and her husband, Chub, were childless and had dedicated their lives to nourishing the orphaned Batschelet children. They had received the red bungalow across from the hotel, which provided the young couple their own space while keeping an eye on Amy's younger siblings. Kate would stay at the hotel for the holidays along with her unmarried sisters Elsie and Trudy. Harry and his wife Cleo had the tree decorated, and a warm glow radiated from within Kate as they approached the three-story structure her father had built many years before. She caught sight of the multicolored lights that shone through the lace curtains of the front parlor, a pleasant observation, celebrating the joy of the season.

The snow was gently falling as Chub caught sight of Harry's headlights and crossed the street to help with Kate's luggage. Amy waved from her porch, announcing that a batch of freshly baked cookies had just come out of the oven and she would be over to the hotel shortly. It was memories like these that drew my parents back to Renovo every year of my childhood. With her suitcases taken up to her old room on the second floor just down the hallway from where she was born, Kate took a few moments to freshen up before Charlie arrived to take her to the Christmas party at the Elks

Club. Stopping in her new niece's nursery to see if she was awake, Kate was pleased to see the little one's big cheeky smile greeting her. Hoping Cleo wouldn't mind, she drew the baby close in her arms, taking in a whiff of the new-born's scent. Then she descended the main stairway. The baby's eyes broadened at the sight of the twinkling colored lights on the tree. Standing in the parlor rocking Susan in her arms, Kate let her gaze sweep over the room. She had come to love this old hotel on the Run. Her childhood had been filled with the bustling activity it provided, its interesting guests always coming and going and the hotel's employees attending to her family.

The front door opened, letting in the chilly night air along with figure of a tall man. Kate admired Charlie's lean, athletic build as he dusted the snow from his coat and boots. The years in the service and as a college basketball player for St. Joseph's in Philadelphia had kept him in good physical shape since high school, though his time spent in the foxholes of Europe had made him a little thinner. As he looked up, their eyes met.

"Hello there, Kate! Is that your new niece?"

"Yes. I hope Cleo doesn't mind, but I wanted to spend some time with her before you arrived."

"That's quite all right, Kate," grinned Cleo as she entered from the hotel's dining room. "I'm sure she wanted to get acquainted with her aunt, too. How are you both? I've been busy in the kitchen with the cook planning Christmas dinner. Can you join us, Charlie?"

"That would be nice, but I have to see what my family has planned, since Mollie is spending the holidays with Harry's family, and Joan is overseas."

"Why don't you bring your parents with you? It would be nice to visit with them, and the hotel can always find room for two more guests."

"That's kind of you, but you know how Mom is uncomfortable socializing outside of the family. By the way, I thought we might stop by to see her on our way to the Club tonight if there's time."

"Let me give this beautiful baby back to her mother and I'll get my coat."

As they left the hotel for the party, the snowflakes had started to fall so fine that Kate wondered if she only imagined them until she felt their presence against her warm cheeks and saw the sparkle as they fell under the glow of the street lamp. They gave the landscape a dusting that looked like sugar coating. Kate and Charlie walked companionably, each caught in quiet reflection.

Wealth and privilege set Kate Batschelet and her family apart from most of the folks in the small mining town. Charlie knew Kate's family's status placed her on a much higher rung of society's ladder, which made his mother uncomfortable. These Old-World values made his plans to ask Kate for her hand in marriage and Bridget's reaction unpredictable. Kate might not even be a welcome guest in his Irish Catholic home; there was such a vast chasm that separated the two in Bridget's eyes. But the past didn't seem as important as the future to Charlie—a future that definitely included Kate.

"Are you sure you want to stop to see your mother tonight?" Kate asked timidly.

"Why not? She has to get used to the idea of us being together one of these days."

"I guess you know her best," answered Kate apprehensively. "But just for a short while; we don't want to be too late."

They parked in front of the rented duplex on Eleventh Street and ascended the painted wooden porch that was slick with snow. Charlie had to support Kate by her elbow as she climbed the steps. Once inside the front door, Kate spotted Hamilton smoking one of his usual roll-ups at the small dining room table with the evening paper. Bridget was in the kitchen baking shortbread; even though she heard them enter, she continued to bake rather than break to greet them. Kate knew this all too well and felt Charlie's uneasiness as they entered the kitchen.

"Hello, Mom. I wanted to stop by before we went to the Elks Club Christmas party so you could see Kate."

"Hello, Mrs. Steen. Your shortbread smells delightful."

"It should, the recipe came all the way from Scotland. It's Hamilton's favorite."

"Kate's brother Harry and his wife Cleo invited us for dinner on Christmas, but I know how you like to be at home on the holidays. It was nice of them to include us up at the hotel, though."

"You were right to excuse us. We celebrate just with our family. A quiet dinner is all we need."

Kate and Charlie exchanged looks and nodded as if hearing what had gone unspoken. Excusing themselves, they left for the party—Bridget not leaving her baking nor Hamilton his paper. Their young romantic life led years ago on the Isle of Wight and London was long forgotten in the years spent forging a life that had brought with it many challenges.

Kate and Charlie spent the evening at the club, filled with holiday merriment socializing with old high school friends. The Elks was decorated inside and out, and a local band pounded out the tunes. Their table choice probably wasn't the best; it comprised of old classmates who had chosen the lifestyle of their parents. This type of future was not in keeping with Kate and Charlie's dreams.

"I'm surprised you chose to grace us common folk with your big-city presence," greeted Betsy, a young woman with two toddlers at home and one on the way. Right after graduation, she had married Jimmy Morgan, an electrician for the railroad. He learned his trade in a class provided by the YMCA. Jimmy and Charlie had been teammates in high school and still shot hoops on breaks from their rail yard jobs. Jimmy had been classified 4F, physically unfit to serve in the war, and this stigma was one that no man wanted during this period of American history. He had been born with one leg considerably shorter than its mate, forcing him to walk with a limp, but it didn't stop his tenacity to play ball. Kate returned Betsy's smile, knowing that her motives to leave Renovo after high school had been instilled deep inside her; she had grown up quickly after the deaths of her parents. Quietly sitting next to Charlie at the table, she realized that her choice to further her education in an out-of-state college had been the right decision for her. Not that she viewed her old friends any less, just differently. It just was not the life for her. They danced until their feet ached and decided to call it a night as the next day was Christmas Eve and everyone had last-minute errands.

Christmas Eve brought light to a cloudless sky with the sun beaming down on the Run. Kate stood at her bedroom window staring at the brightness of the day. The promise of warmth brought about by the intensity of the sunshine was ill founded. The snow crunched beneath her footfalls, and her breath all but froze in midair as she crossed the road and entered her sister Amy's garden gate. A path encircled the bungalow in a crescent to the back porch where Kate entered a kitchen filled with the aroma of Amy's baking. Since she had grown up years ahead of her time, Kate's insight had always been guided by Amy's motherly ways. She had been interested in success and scholarship, while not enough in the divine as Amy was. Drawing her attention to the present, she sought her sister's advice.

"Hey there, Sis!"

"Well, you finally got up after a night out partying with Charlie," greeted Amy in her maternal voice.

"It was great fun—I saw all sorts of friends home for the holidays. Do you have time to talk while you bake?"

"Sure, Honey; is everything all right?"

"I think so. I think Charlie may ask me to marry him tonight. It's just an intuition, but his mother doesn't seem to approve of me."

"Why would she not approve? You're from a prominent family of good moral values and have your own career."

"That's just the reason; her Old-World values come from when she worked as a servant to Princess Beatrice. The Victorian society she was accustomed to was very class-conscious; everyone married within his or her own economic level. She views us as the wealthy and above them, and having my own career doesn't help."

"But her daughters are nurses."

"Yes, but she feels that fits into what's acceptable—

being a housewife, mother, cook, housekeeper or caring for the ill as the princess had done during the War, not a college instructor."

"Don't let her scare you with her textures of domesticity."

"I know I shouldn't, but she does. I had always hoped if I got married that my mother-in-law would be like a mother to me with Mom gone, but I am glad I have you." Giving her sister a hug, they shared in the loss of that empty space their parents had once filled.

On that night in the parlor of the West Branch Hotel, Charlie presented Kate with an engagement ring that she lovingly accepted. He wrapped her in his arms; they fit so well together as she snuggled the top of her head be-

What we learn through life experiences is imprinted on the next generation. Our gift of life and the true meaning of the battles we have faced.

neath his chin. He declared, "You are the woman I want to be with. If that means leaving these mountains I will gladly go as long as you're with me."

At that moment, a roar of applause exploded in the adjoining hotel dining room. The young couple was unaware the family had been eavesdropping. Harry pulled out a bottle of champagne and they toasted the proposal as all in the hotel celebrated a festive Christmas Eve in 1947. Thus the imprints my parents held within their DNA were about to pass on to the next generation.

14

Life Travels On

Iam a product of the sandwich generation; I was caught between my children and aging parents, some sixty-four years after that Christmas Eve when my father asked for my mother's hand in marriage. Eight years out from my last treatment, I am currently in remission. As I previously divulged, I am now dealing with two meningioma brain tumors. Continuing to go in for checkups—usually every six to twelve months either for the present tumors or previous cancers—has its continual highs and lows as I approach a checkup or wait for the results. This waiting game plays havoc on the emotions and psychological elements I continue to face in over-the-hill middle age. My role as a survivor is forever changing. Hoping to come to grips with my past cancers and uncertain future with brain tumors, at the urging of a friend I became motivated to share my world to help patients stricken with critical illness to realize they are not alone. In keeping with

My parents' wedding

that promise, I have spoken to varied audiences on my devotion to the Divine Mercy and how it came about, but I hadn't written about my life as a survivor, caregiver to elderly parents, and victim of brain tumors. Since I have been placed in stressful situations over the past several years, I have tried to maintain my position as a wife, mother, and daughter, though not always up to the standards I would have liked. My new brain tumors are physically making the risk of falling affect some of my capabilities.

Under these situations I recently elected to undergo a test to see if the problems I had been having with the functioning of my left leg might be the result of my spinal scoliosis and not the tumors. The doctors at Mayo informed me that the operation to remove the largest brain tumor holds such a high risk of death or paralysis that at this point, surgery isn't an option. My hope was that my spine, which had caused me to lose three inches in height since college, had compacted and compressed a nerve. Through exercise or physical therapy I might be able to regain better control of my leg and foot. At present I find myself at times walking as though I am drunk and unsteady. I can't walk a straight line drawn on the pavement. I had thought this was just a part of aging when I would lose my balance. Meningiomas are very slow-growing tumors, eighty percent of which, like mine, are noncancerous. Your body, I have found, has an unbelievable capability to adjust to tumors growing inside of it. That is why some cancers are so hard to detect before they are very advanced. This is why regular tests such as mammograms and self-breast exams are so important.

To see me battle and survive the disease gave my daughters and countless other children at their school a level of sensitivity and provided a different perspective toward the possibility of survival and the miracles God can grace us with.

At nine o'clock one summer morning I underwent a hideous and excruciating test without anesthesia. It required large needles with attached electrodes inserted in my legs to measure my impulses. The doctor performing the procedure would twist and turn the needles to see what impulses the electronic charges would send into the legs. This resulted in horrible sensations. Undergoing this test I envisioned a prisoner at the hands of some evil interrogator who was shining a blinding light in his victim's eyes as he tortured him with electric shocks. How could I have put myself through this! It is amazing what you will do when you seek a cure. Did I really need to know that badly? Was the awkwardness of a weak left leg and foot something I could just live with? Most of us gaining in years deal with different adversities as our body parts age. In fact, I had noticed this weakness earlier in the year and just attributed my clumsiness to age. Why had the knowledge of my tumors prompted me to undergo such a test? Should I not be just happy to be alive? All these questions and more rushed through my head as I lay on this table with needles in my legs. As it was, the test results yielded no nerve involvement; thus the tumors were the culprits. "Oh well, just live with it, Sue," I console myself.

Each patient is an individual, "there is no one size fits all." Too often in an effort to find answers and save time, generalities are made. As my friend, Pam, and I proved, the prognosis can be wrong. There is no benefit to slotting patients into statistics that appear to fit or to refer to "just a stage" that a cancer victim or survivor may be passing through. Each of us is so different, with so many factors playing within this battle, that the stage syndrome may obscure what is really happening inside us. In my journey, my feelings were mine and mine alone as were Pam's, Gale's, Heidi's, Uncle Red's, Jeanne's, and endless numbers of victims. Knowing that it is normal didn't change what I felt or eliminate my pain.

I found many people needed to compare my cancer to someone they knew who had suffered from the disease. Their denseness and lack of sensitivity was shocking as they divulged information that was totally inappropriate or had negative results. I didn't want to hear about their poor Aunt Martha who died of complications during surgery or their mother who became incapacitated due to her brain tumors. The total detachment people express through their ignorance is amazing. For this reason, when I feel sorry for my girls having to live through this disease with me, I remind myself of the experience they have gained. To see me battle and survive the disease gave them and countless other children at their school a level of sensitivity and provided a different perspective toward the possibility of survival and the miracles God can grace us with.

To compare victims can deny them their own uniqueness. Each case is different, as is each individual. Treatment can be chosen on a hypothesis of similar cases, but each illness is unique. I once asked my oncologist if he had ever dealt with a patient who had as many primary cancers as me and his answer was "yes!" One of his patients had eight! My three didn't look all that bad after I heard that.

At times I would drift to thoughts of what it would have been like if I had battled the disease at a different time or place. What would my chance of survival have been like years before or years in the future? There are no sure answers to many illnesses, only hypotheses. Most cases cannot be linked to just one provocation but a combination. To search for a reason to place blame would serve me no purpose. Only through my faith will I be allowed to accept my circumstances and the opportunity to make my life more meaningful from this point on. Society needs to look beyond the outward signs of hair loss and disfiguring scars to the individual spirit that lives within the soul of the cancer victim.

Sometimes people have a way of dealing with diseases, like cancer, that they don't understand, by supporting theories that happy people without stresses don't get cancer. We cannot always prevent the disease through personality, but it does help the victim psychologically to deal with the situation and readjust their lives. In an attempt to not add more stress to an already upsetting situation, I expressed little anger toward my disease or the battles I was waging. "Seeking proven methods according to Dawson Church by way of shifting our emotional balance towards happiness, we initiate the epigenetic signals that shift our gene expression toward health."[10]

Mr. Church goes on to state in his book *The Genie In Your Genes* that Epigenetics—control of the genes from outside the cell—is a brand new branch of science that promises a revolution in health and happiness. Exciting new scientific research shows that genes are being turned on and off—every day—by your beliefs, feelings, and attitudes. Every thought ripples throughout your body, affecting your immune system, brain, and hormones.[11]

In an attempt to fulfill demands placed on me by society, those I love, and my own personal goals, I fear I am still weak in valuing the true importance of life in an effort to attain that which I seek in my eternity. Did it really take the death of my parents to make me face the reality of life and take a close look at myself, reflecting on how my grandchildren and their children may one day look back at me?

I have to ask myself, "Do I take too many good times

---

10 Church, Dawson. *The Genie In Your Genes* (Energy Psychology Press, Santa Rosa, CA 95403 2009) p. 329
11 Ibid.

for granted? Is my present state all too often absorbed with looking at what I feel is wrong in this life? Do I forget back when I feared I would never see the life I am living today?" I find myself rushing through my days one moment to the next, not reflecting on how I am changing. Life cannot be valued in how we survive it but in how we *live* it. My illness taught me the value of being alive, and the fear of death restores that value. In my need to seek the proper proportion of what I value in my life, I realized that I need to respect my illness and honor death. I witnessed my mother's death after she was placed in hospice care, coincidentally in the same room and same bed in which my father had died three years prior. It was for them a conclusion in the last chapter to a beautiful marriage.

> *My illness taught me the value of being alive, and the fear of death restores that value.*

While writing this book I was granted the opportunity to travel the breathtaking countryside of Austria and see the city of Salzburg, the site of the filming of *The Sound of Music*. The 1965 film written by Ernest Lehman was based an autobiography of Maria von Trapp entitled *The von Trapp Family Singers*. At one point in the movie, Reverend Mother of the Abbey says, "When the Lord closes a door, somewhere He opens a window." This can be said for the journey of experiences a terminally ill patient travels.

I cry for those souls who have not known our Lord and have not been born in the waters of baptism into the faith and also for souls who do not know the joy and fullness of giving and receiving the Lord and His love for mankind.

It is through this journey in my battle with cancer that I have witnessed the change inside myself; I have come to realize that I am alive today not for selfishness of self, but to pay witness to the grace the Lord has given me. I faced a challenge and only through the gift of "free will" could I meet my challenge to be here today.

I do not believe when we are born that our path is made for us. I believe God has given us graces with our birth and one of those is "free will" to use as our weapon against evil. Yet it is up to us how and if we chose to use it. It is through proper use of that will that we can fulfill our destiny into eternity. I lived beyond all expectation with the grace of God. Even with all the economic funds and care at my disposal, when death lingers at the end of the journey they are but flimsy shields next to faith.

As I deal with my pride that refuses the use of a cane at this time, I worry about the day that may inevitably come when my left leg will refuse to lift from the ground to take a step. It may go dead and limp as it did on a hot late summer day two years ago. As autumn approached, I was in my garden deadheading the summer flowers that had seen their last fruitful days as they stood with only brown, wilted petals. On that day, the physical experience of losing all feeling in my leg lasted but a few short minutes but produced the scare of a family trait where stroke played an integral part of aging. The same condition had overcome my two aunts and mother, so it prompted me to divulge the incident at my yearly physical the following week. The prescribed CT test was familiar to me, one I was all too accustomed to.

The results came as a shock, and I was once again hurled into a spine-chilling fog, not knowing what evil lurked in the shadows of the scan. The test showed two brain tumors with unclear origins. Had my prior cancers metastasized to my brain or were these tumors unrelated? A trip to Mayo provided no results and only time would give us an answer. If they were cancerous, the end would come quickly; if not, there were no crystal balls showing my future travels. I was living one day at a time, and confusion hit me as all my unanswered questions could find no explanation. Nothing could dilute my urgent need to know where I was headed. My fate was in the hands of the Almighty. If the risk was too great to be healed by the surgeon's knife, then I had to continue on my quest for meaning in the time I had left.

The time from when the visual images of the tumors appeared on the CT until now has proven that I surely am not dying anytime soon. I'm constantly searching for new ways to battle the emotional turmoil I face with an unknown future as these tumors remain present. I must pass my time from the sidelines, not able to battle, but only watch what may be in store. I deal with my short-term memory faltering and my leg growing weaker, the result of which may be coupled with this imprinted soul growing older. I face the weakness of a body affected by age and these ever-present brain tumors.

My past thirteen years as a cancer patient and survivor has been an eye-opening and soul-searching experience. I am still reentering my life as I view it from the position as a survivor and as a patient dealing with new experiences. Often acquaintances—casual and long-standing—will approach me to check out my latest survival saga. The recurring comment usually stems from how well I am looking. To this I find myself shuddering inside. You may ask yourself why would I feel as such? The result comes from an age-old internal conflict that resonates from a superstitious nature. I remember times when my lost comrades in this war for survival would appear to be improving right before they took a turn for the worst and the feeling of fear that a battle would return once again.

I have also become leery of questions about my health issues unless they are motivated by genuine concern. It is amazing how many people have fallen to the ills of society by way of enjoyment, interest, or curiosity seeking to witness catastrophes of another human being. It reminds me of television viewers who notoriously watch the evening news to live their lives through others' ill fortunes, patting themselves on the backs for being so lucky in avoiding such situations. To those feeble souls who fit this sorrowful description, I offer a heartfelt cry to give of yourself so that you may truly live in the pain of the suffering and take from it the true experience of life. For if I were to value my years since my first diagnosis against my innocent first forty-two years, I would have to truthfully say my last have been more bountiful. I have witnessed miracles, lived in my faith more closely, and bettered myself by confronting my weaknesses and trying to deal with them. All of it has been self-enlightening through the experiences I have lived. There are no substitutions for the experience of touching life by way of a serious illness, either through your own life or as a caregiver.

Being able to share the cancer battle with those we love makes it bearable. When our caregivers, family, and friends recognize our pain, it reduces the suffering. I cannot explain why—only that it is fundamental in the battle. Society places demands on the caregiver, sometimes not realizing in most cases that person is also a bread-winner and having to take on extra duties as though a single parent.

Being able to share the cancer battle with those we love makes it bearable. When our caregivers, family, and friends recognize our pain, it reduces the suffering.

Rebuilding a life after cancer can be as hard as the economic stresses a victim faces waging his or her war against the disease. Cancer victims may face employers who only look at them in respect to their work value and productiveness. Some ignore the need to attend to an illness in the hopes of returning to work at a later date and earn a profitable income. Survivors make valuable employees; the cancer may have granted them experience to make them better team players or leaders.

The victim can talk of living through the battle but it is not as easily expressed for the caregiver. This I learned first-hand when my parents moved in with us after my mother's stroke. Following the natural tendency of society, everyone seemed to forget about my recovery period. I had always seemed to bounce back, while on the inside the wound was fresh and deep. It may have been my way of trying to shove aside the cancer by jumping into another battle. At this time I was only one year out from my third cancer. I was a recovering survivor, caregiver, mother, wife, and daughter all rolled into one stressed-out human being.

My days consisted of carpooling either to one school for grades kindergarten through eighth grade some twenty minutes away or my oldest daughter's high school thirty minutes away. This was followed by household errands, then returning home by lunchtime to feed my parents and throw in a load of laundry, which was never-ending with seven people. My parents' doctors' appointments, blood counts, and physical therapies usually consumed my afternoons. Then I was off to one of the two schools for pick-up time. By the time I got back I had to start dinner, eat, and cleanup with the help of the girls before returning to one of the schools for volleyball or basketball practice. I usually collapsed into bed around eleven after I shuffled more laundry between the washer and dryer and did a last-minute check on my parents to see if they needed anything.

I was trying to be everything to everyone, guilt ridden by what I had put my family through during the previous five years of battling my illness. Now when they needed me I was falling apart. I had taken on too much too quickly in an effort to avoid my weaknesses. In doing so, the recovery has been even longer and harder. The deaths of both of my parents within four years followed another dimension to the journey into survival—an emotional journey to seek out peace through the purging of my experiences.

Let time follow its own path with your recovery as you survive through this disease. Give yourself time; ignore the impatience of others who want you to quickly return to your old life as they feel you should. That path is probably not the journey you may choose, as you are not nor will ever be that same person again. In this you may mourn as those of us mourn the physical features of youth growing older and watching our body age. Yet, we possess the wisdom in our wrinkles that cannot be erased—at least erased "naturally." After surviving cancer you have earned this time; take a deep breath and enjoy it. Take comfort in watching the sunrise on a spring morning, a walk in the flaming foliage of an autumn day, or the crystal sparkle of a freshly fallen snow. Treat yourself, for God has given you this splendor.

There is grief in the circumstances you have just endured, and this battle can teach you the worth in the experience. As you endure the loss of your old way of life you will find the value in this new one if you take the time to smell the sweet perfume of survival.

My life has led me to believe that through this journey there is urgent need to fight—not flee—when it comes down to the purest of form of survival. It is your life and you must find value in the experience at all costs. Whether the result of your survival is nature or nurture through the imprint of your human genome, the person you are and the behavioral traits you possess or can possess is up to the use of the "free will" that God has graced you with. You can now be that proud warrior of a hard-fought battle, one who is admired by those who pay witness to your battle. Or you can be a coward, but it is up to you and you alone. Through survival you will learn a lesson you will need to share with those around you. They will try to get you to return to your old self. That endeavor will be a losing battle; it is like a parent trying to hold a teenager at bay. As a young adult you must experience life to mature; as a cancer survivor you must experience your battles with illness to go on. Young adults will never be able to return to the childish lives they once led prior to achieving adulthood, as you will never be able to return to the innocence of your pre-cancer years. This is not a punishment but a rite of passage into the imprinted survivor you can become within remission. It was not a time in space where I started to arrange feelings of insanity in a sane pattern in my life. It was a place in time when my feelings truly developed into a coherent logical pattern that resembled a future. I found myself in a place where I had to break away from my past to embrace the future. It wasn't an easy road to travel; I become aware of the distinguishing behavioral characteristics that separate the survivors and the victims.

For any survivors to have a chance at a future they must learn to abandon the worn-out lives they lived in search of new ones. I now try to map out a new path to follow in my future as I travel forward toward a reinvention of this life. I am altered from the experiences I have endured as my views have formed new shapes. These shapes are still dimensionally similar in their state yet uniquely new in their own right. Molded from being pulled and kneaded as if a piece of clay in a potter's hand, they are transformed into a totally new piece of art. It is reminiscent of the artist's techniques, yet developing into an entirely new expression of the experience.

My future holds a new light in this way. It resembles my old self visually. Sue on the outside, just inching past mid-life into my later years. Our children are almost out on their own in careers and spreading their wings in educational college endeavors. Joe and I are facing a more quiet time in our lives, hopefully to reconnect and grow old together. We are in a place in time that may change or stay the same, but one that has been transformed after our past twenty-five years on this bumpy road raising our three daughters and battling cancer as husband and wife. Yet even though I try to envision this slower-paced way of life as my promising future, the fear of facing my aging years with reduced physical and mental capabilities terrifies me. Not in the same way that my illness did, but from the position that it is a natural way of life and one to be accepted. Even though many have fought to keep their youth through surgical procedures, deals with the devil are as farfetched as fictional vampires; aging has a degree of insanity built within it. I have known very few individuals who just flowed slowly downstream to a natural death. Either their life was taken too soon or was lived through extreme harshness, stressed by either physical or emotional pain or both. Unless through the dear Lord's graces they were born of a simple mind or chose to use their "free will" to a higher spiritual level, a precise level that guided them to eternal salvation and peace. Humans are not usually born with this peace; it is an acquired state achieved by traveling into a chasm of great despair and out again, as one would travel through a labyrinth. Living the experience is once again the key.

The years since my diagnosis in 1998 represent a long and fruitful journey. I have traced my ancestral heritage to its Epigenetic roots; become the product of superb doctors whose technical craft, judgment, and spirit have guided me through chemo and surgery; benefited from the aid of countless friends and family; been prayed for by endless souls; found

As you endure the loss of your old way of life you will find the value in this new one if you take the time to smell the sweet perfume of survival.

theological guidance from wonderful clergy and ministries; discovered the strength to fight; and above all have
been graced by God through a devotion in my heart—a
heart of a grateful woman.

My storytelling is confessional. Like my art, it paints
a picture of my soul with its entire candor, a mix of who
I am and who I want to be. I travel to my private inner
place where my soul can be exposed, naked in all its flaws,
where only I can create alterations in its imperfections by
way of my imaginary paint and brush, thus transforming
it into a beautiful image for all to witness in my person. In
this inner place inside my soul I find comfort with all its
familiar ways and creativeness. I have emerged from this
place to face the author's world, leaving behind an artist's
creative memoir and growing in my new experiences that
share in narration, a story I must concede to tell.

My story does not resemble the beautiful wonders of
nature in the sky, mountains, lakes, trees, and flowers of
my past paintings, but of the nature in cells dividing un-
controllably, leaving this victim gasping for my body to
be rid of this deadly illness. A world filled with drinking
too much coffee and out-of-control mindless expansion
into my journey to gather up my hopes and dreams that
I failed to divulge in the past for lack of proper verbiage.
With prayers I retreat to my devotion to see a future free
of blight and disease, a future we victims of survival snarl
at, as we bite and claw our way to some form of remission.
It is not a pretty picture to gaze at from that viewpoint,
but then life is here to be lived and experienced to the
fullest capacity, not just to be observed from the sidelines.

Mine is a dimension sometimes void of reason, since at

present I'm sharing my brain mass with two tumors. There are days that I seek to find the words to describe what I wish to convey. Days filled with a haze I can only compare to empty confusion. Days that find me so disorientated I envision myself traveling in concentric circles, as my grandmother's tear in her teacup, trying to break out of a confusion that is holding me firmly in its grasp. Today I once again stumbled as my left foot didn't quite clear the step riser; unable to break my fall, I landed on my right knee leaving it badly bruised and bloody. I hope to start an acceptance of my newfound weaknesses in this battle as I journey down life's path of yet more experiences to befriend.

I try to maintain my dignity and decorum in the insanity I feel. I try to derive some comfort from the thought of creating stories of my ancestral heritage and the epigenetic gene pool to which I belong, a bloodline that flows through my veins and is shared with my forefathers. It is for this reason I have come to my father's beloved northern lakefront cabin in the north woods of Michigan in the summer of 2011. Sitting at his roll-top desk, I can view the morning's dawn as it rises in hues of pale gold and mauve over the still glassiness of the water's surface. The distinct call of a lone loon flows over the stillness of the lake as if the bird and I are the only creatures present in this distant moment in time. Sipping my freshly brewed morning coffee and trying to dig into past memories, I have come to my "On Golden Pond." Here is a place to reconnect with my soul and find some peace of mind in contrast to the hectic life I lead in the city. Dad shared my passion for gardening, possibly inherited from his mother Bridget's love of the rose gardens she planted on the Isle of Wight and behind her rented duplexes in her small town in the Allegheny Mountains.

Gazing down to the water's edge from my laptop I can see the wild mint and delicate blue forget-me-nots Dad planted. They call to me of times long gone, when I would spend hours fishing off our weathered dock, endlessly snagging the branches of the old oak that grew on the shoreline. As I tried to perfect my cast, the oak would catch my hooks gone astray, and I would call for Dad to help retrieve my fishing line so I could continue. Without ever losing patience,

We are not born with this peace; it is an acquired state achieved by traveling into a chasm of great despair and out again. Living the experience is the key.

he would come to my aid again and again. This memory brings me back to that time when I started this journey and searched through my old chest looking for answers to my lineage and realizing I have few if any relatives past the age of eighty who can provide answers to my questions. I now have arrived, here in the Great North Woods, which Dad called "God's Country," to finish my journey. I once heard this place described as a piece of heaven, a small chasm in this enormous hemisphere where I feel at home.

The ties that bind me to my past are strong as I struggle with the impending years when my body must be laid to rest and my soul will long for the peninsula between the two bays in my northern state. I pray to God for comfort in the heartfelt knowledge that He is my home and where my soul should be in the nonphysical world of eternity.

Why am I so driven to find answers to questions in my past and soul at this time in my life? Am I like the salmon driven to swim upstream to spawn in the land from whence they came and then die? Returning now to the city by the bay in the woods of Northern Michigan, I will regenerate my battery, growing weak from lack of recent charging at the old homestead on the lake. Searching for a force deep within my soul that constantly beckons my return to the north, I am driven with no second thought to ever look back to the city from which I have come. I'm immersed in the need to draw from a place where I can touch the cool spring waters, smell the pines, taste the sweet cherries, see the wondrous sunsets, and hear the sounds of katydids and woodpeckers. I come to be in my father's place. Here is a small oasis where I feel my epigenetic roots. I can communicate with him through our ties to this retreat, which he created in an old cabin nestled in the pines on a spring-feed lake. In this I am drawn to seek out the swiftly flowing waters he so enjoyed in his favorite trout-fishing stream down by Brown Bridge Road. I recall his recollections of the similarity of this stream to his crystal mountain-fed creeks up in the Allegheny Mountains of Pennsylvania where he came as a young immigrant boy and left as a man. He risked his life against the evil ways of Adolf Hitler and returned a changed soul, one who grew immeasurably though his war experiences. My cancer allowed me to share an understanding with my father I could never have without the disease. Coming face to face with death, as he had in the Hardt Mountains of 1945, gave us the ability to view the reality of mortality. He witnessed this reality in the eyes of Dachau, which brought hope to the vision in the need to fight not flee. In those separate experiences we were able to unite our souls in a manner we never could have without such trials. We had been to that place where you see your life come before your eyes and wonder about the survival of it all. Sharing in such experiences in each of our private wars and emerging better for it, Dad and I went on to spend the quality time we had left to share. The big regret was my own weakness, as I witnessed my big strong Irish Scotch father weaken to the illness of old age and wither away. I avoided seeing what was right before my eyes as I could not and would never see weakness in my fighter, who will always remain a great man in my eyes.

The finality of death came to me in the passing of my comrades in the cancer battle, but slapped me in the face for the first time in the grief of my parents' deaths. I struggle today, distancing the finality in the feeling of closeness I receive from familiar surroundings I will always call home. I feel their souls are near, watching over me. But most of all I share in their epigenetic trait to fight for what I believe holds value, the greatest being "free will." I seek to possess free will in my life as it holds the infinite key to our imprinted survival.

All Christians bond to their faith as they commit to shared beliefs by emotional connection. In my religious fellowship, I found unity that gave me strength. The word "religion" comes from the Latin *religare*, or to bind. This bond or binding may have been the basis that formed societies and linked genetic criteria. I have come to find in religion's intricate and complex role within our ancestral history there are strong emotional ties that shape the religious behavior within each of us.

15

A Song of Mercy

s I presently travel over this bumpy road through life—not to mention the huge chuckholes I drive over on a never-ending journey—I try to follow God's GPS up my present middle-aged mountain. I remember the Sunday following Easter in the year 2000 when Pope John Paul canonized Sister Faustina to sainthood, and I think about the devotion to the Divine Mercy, which she helped make the world aware of through her diary. In the diary she describes her visions from Jesus and the message of Divine Mercy. Three times that day, the Pope supported this call to be the message for the third millennium, to all people, as "God's gift to our time. In light of this twofold canonization, and the condition of the world," Pope John Paul II expressed a strong urgency about turning to God's mercy "now, while there is still time for mercy...as the people of this restless time of ours are wavering between the emptiness of self-exaltation and the humiliation of despair."[12]

---

12 Kosicki, Rev. George W. *Living the Divine Mercy* (Our Sunday Vistor, Inc., Huntington, Indiana, 2008) pp. 8-9

According to Pope John Paul II in a quote of Jesus' own words to St. Faustina, "Mankind will not have peace until it turns with trust to My mercy."[13] The love of one's brothers and sisters are inseparable, make St. Faustina's beautiful exclamation your own, **"Jesus, I trust in you."**

Painting by Susan, 2001

I am currently searching for ways to spread the word of the importance that we Christians educate ourselves on suffering, survival, and the trust we place in our Lord along with the grace He has given us in the ability to use our "free will." I am working to help victims of cancer believe in miracles because they really do happen. If that is not God's will, your soul's eternity is worth the battle you will find in the peace and strength gained in the devotion to the "Divine Mercy."

With that in mind, I share the work of Vinny Flynn and *MercySong*. Vinny is known to many as "the man who

---

13 Diary: St. Maria Faustina Kowalska, *Divine Mercy in My Soul* (Congregation of Marians of the Immaculate Conception, Stockbridge, MA 1987). p. 300.

sings the Divine Mercy Chaplet on EWTN," including myself when I was first stricken with lung cancer in 1998. In fact, I was listening to Vinny and his family while reciting my chaplet on that first Friday in July when the call came from my doctor's office informing me of the miracle of my cancer's disappearance. You can imagine my excitement when my parish priest, Father William Ashbaugh, asked me to take on the responsibility of Vinny's visit to our parish in 2001. At that time I was dealing with my second remission and looked forward to meeting Vinny and his family. Since my promise to spread the word of the devotion, I had been educating the children in our parish on the history behind St. Faustina and leading the chaplet on Fridays in our church.

Vinny Flynn has been involved in a ministry of mercy for over thirty years, using his gifts of teaching, writing, counseling, music, and prayer to help people understand the teachings of the Church and open their hearts to the healing touch of God's love. A former Executive Editor at the Marian Helpers Center and former General Manager of Divine Mercy International, Vinny was actively involved in spreading the message of Divine Mercy, presenting workshops for religious and lay leaders, and writing or editing various Divine Mercy publications.

In 1993, Vinny and his wife Donna, with all seven of their children involved in music and ministry, established a recording/publishing company to produce and distribute their family music CDs, talks on tape, and religious publications.

In 2003, the family ministries were incorporated under the name MercySong, Inc. as a 501c(3) Catholic not-for-profit organization dedicated to bringing healing to others by leading them to personal experience of the Father's love through music, teaching, counseling, and prayer.[14]

Since our first meeting in 2001, Vinny and his wife Donna have graced my family with periodic visits. During such times they have allowed me to sponsor them as my guests when they visit our parish community and most recently my oldest daughter's college, Madonna University, as a guest speaker. Without the Divine Mercy Devotion I may not have the life I am graced with today. I encourage you to visit the ministry's website at www.mercysong.com to learn more about this wonderful ministry and all it has to offer on the devotion and healing those of us who struggle with the battles we face in life.

In my faith I trust.
In my blessings I am thankful.
In my experiences I am graced.
In my life I have seen survival.
Above all, in my soul I have found meaning.

---

14 Flynn, Vinny, *7 Secrets of the Eucharist* (Mercysong, Inc. Stockbridge, Massachusetts USA 2006). p. 131

Conclusion

As we near the end in this journey, I find that my answer is an explanation not just of the imprint I have received from my ancestors, but of the strength all people possess within their souls. A strength that we human beings can grasp on to in our battles and give a good fight, whatever our heritage. We can possess an imprint to have the strength to endure until the last breath, for God has given all of us the "free will," and with that we make our choices. Our battles are not won on battlefields; they are won on operating tables, with chemo and radiation treatments, many tears, and a whole lot of prayers. We strive to endure graciously for our family and friends and for ourselves that we may hold our heads high as we stroll down life's path. What a rollercoaster of a ride it can be. Hopefully the next generations we will imprint shall praise the lives we have led, and our memory will have its own story to tell.

Acknowledgments

The Imprinted Survivor is a Spiritual Christian Memoir seeking to give the reader insight into the battles one faces dealing with cancer, while creatively incorporating a bounty of historical facts. Set at times on England's Isle of Wight and the city of London, it then travels to the Allegheny Mountains of Pennsylvania. Readers join the author in search of the inner strength to survive possibly inherited through personality traits of ancestors long deceased.

Due to the time frame of early to mid-1900s I hope that my ancestors and cousins do not take offense to the narrative liberties that I have taken in conversations based on tales told to me. I have sought to document historical facts, and sources can be found in the bibliography. Luckily Dad left an extensive memoir, and his sister Mollie took the time to share with him letters of correspondence she found between Grandmother and the royal household along with pictures. Aunt Amy, Mom's oldest sister, who also shared my interest in ancestry, spent endless hours with her cousins, Claire and "Rusty" Manning, on the Manning Family Tree, which supported my maternal family's research. Their documentation allowed me to join The Daughters of the American Revolution, Philip Livingston Chapter NSDAR.

I cannot forget my patient editor, Erin Howarth, big thank yous for reading and editing my various errors. Without your wonderful ability and knowledge of *The Book of Kells, The Imprinted Survivor* would not have such beautiful Celtic Font and cover design. You were a saint to cope so graciously with my crazy e-mails. My wonderful friend Jonnie Bryant at McNaughton & Gunn, Inc. for your wonderful encouragement to create this book and seeing it to completion.

To Micki, the closest person I have to a sister. Even though we do not share the same epigenetics, I am so thankful to have you and your family—Ken, Robert, and Megan—within my extended family. Your help and support has been relentless through all my battles.

I would also like to extend my appreciation to author and educator Wayne Short for his research into Renovo's history and the Renovo Library for their efforts to help ancestors gather research information through their microfilm archive. My cousin Dianne, whose enthusiasm I cannot forget, spurred me to delve even deeper into our family's legacy.

I need to give special thanks to my family and friends, who organized dinners, babysitting and carpools to help our family through the roughest of times. I cannot thank

Mary, my Polish mother-in-law, enough for passing on her heritage and faith through introducing me to Saint Faustina. To Marybeth for all your unending companionship, spiritual support not to mention computer savvy, that helped make this creative endeavor much more efficient. My special people: my sister-in-law Bernadette, Aunt Mary, and friends Holly, Judy, Angie, and Pam for your unconditional friendship and support. Not to mention all the wonderful care afforded me by my oncologist, surgeon and general practitioner whose knowledge and bedside manner made the journey possible.

Bless you Father John and Father Bill for your dedication and love of your faith and parishioners. And Vinny Flynn and your family who gave inspiration to my devotion to the Divine Mercy.

Finally, I owe much to my husband, Joseph, whose love, strength and positive attitude was my rock through these illnesses. My girls Sarah, Abbey, and Frannie, the next generation, who survived my journey and have given me much joy in witnessing their growth into the beautiful Christian women, to whom I dedicate this book.

Bibliography

BOOKS

Adam, James Truslow, *The Epic of America* (Little, Boston, 1931)

Church, Dawson, *The Genie In Your Genes* (Energy Psychology Press, Santa Rosa, CA, 2009)

Dennison, Matthew, *The Last Princess* (St. Martin Press, New York, 2007)

Duff, David, *The Shy Princess* (Fredrick Muller Ltd., London, 1974)

Glardi, Julia P. *Born to Rule* (St. Martin Press, New York, 2005)

Hughes, Kristine, *Everyday Life in Regency and Victorian England* (Writer's Digest Books, Cincinnati, Ohio, 1998)

Kowalska, St. Maria Faustina, *Diary: Divine Mercy In My Soul* (Congregation of Marians of the Immaculate Conception, Stockbridge MA, 1987)

Manning, William, *The Key of Libberty* [Sic](The Manning Association, Billerica, Massachusetts, 1922)

May, Trevor, *The Victorian Domestic Servant* (Shire Publications Ltd, Buckinghamshire, UK, 2002)

McNie, Alan, *Clan Sinclair* (Cascade Publishing Company, Jedburg, Scotland, 1986)

O'Brien, Tim, *The Things They Carried* (Houghton Mufflin Harcourt Publishing Company, New York, 1990)

Packard, Jerrold M., *Victoria's Daughters* (St. Martin Press, New York, 1998)

Short, Wayne E., *The History of Renovo, Pennsylvania* (1926-1950)

Tennant, Connie, *East Cowes A Step into the Past* (1992)

Wade, Nicholas, *Before The Dawn* (The Penguin Press, New York, 2006)

Wade, Nicholas, *The Faith Instinct* (The Penguin Press, New York, 2009)

MAGAZINES

Discover Magazine, "DNA Is Not Destiny" by Ethan Watters. http://discovermagazine.com/2006//nov/cover/article_view?b_start:int=3&-C

Newsweek, "Sins of the Grandfathers" by Sharon Begley. November 8, 2010

Time Magazine, "Epigenetics, DNA: How You Can Change Your Genes, Destiny" http://www.time.com/time/health/article/0,8599,1951968,00.htm

WEBSITES

Goleman, Daniel. "Major Personality Study Finds That Traits Are Mostly Inherited."The New York Times. December 2, 1986 http://www.nytimes.com/1986/12/02/secience/major-personality-study-finds-that-traits-are-...

Hunter, Phillip. "What Genes Remember." Prospect Magazine. May24, 2008-Issue 146 http://www.prospect-magazine.co.uk/2008/05/whatgenesremember/

Kasson S. Joy. www.dit.ncssm.edu/lmtm/docs/Uprooted/finalscript.pdf.

"Epigentics, DNA: How You Can Change Your Genes, Destiny" http://www.time.com/time/health/article/0,8599,1951968,00.html

Kowalska, St. Maria Faustina. Diary: Divine Mercy In My Soul. Online www.marian.org.

"Labyrinth – Intro." http://www.labyrinth.org.uk/

Lupu, Alexandra. "Our Personality – Is It Genetically Inherited or Determined by The Enviromental Factors?" Softpedia. July 2, 2006 http://news.softpedia.com/news/Our-Personality-Is- It- Genetically-Inherited-or-Determined...

Miller, Ilana. "Victorian Era." www.victorianpast.com/FrontPorch/victorianera.htm

Ritberger, Carol. "Personality…Its In The Genes." In Light Times. Oct. 1998 <http://www.inlightimes.com/archives/1998/10/personality.htm>

Siebert, Al PhD. "The Survivor Personality."Practical Psychology Press.http://www.practicalpsychologypress.com/titles/chotsp.shtml

"The Home Front." Ask.com. http://www.historylearningsite.co.uk/home_front_1914_to_1918.ht